Teaching What Matters Most

Standards and Strategies for Raising Student Achievement

Richard W. Strong,
Harvey F. Silver, and
Matthew J. Perini

ASCD

Association for Supervision and Curriculum Development
Alexandria, Virginia USA

Association for Supervision and Curriculum Development
1703 N. Beauregard St. • Alexandria, VA 22311-1714 USA
Telephone: 1-800-933-2723 or 703-578-9600 • Fax: 703-575-5400
Web site: http://www.ascd.org • E-mail: member@ascd.org

Printed in the United States of America.

August 2001 member book (p). ASCD Premium, Comprehensive, and Regular members periodically receive ASCD books as part of their membership benefits. No. FY01-09.

ASCD Product No. 100057
ASCD member price: $18.95   nonmember price: $22.95

Library of Congress Cataloging-in-Publication Data
Strong, Richard W., 1946–
    Teaching what matters most : standards and strategies for raising student achievement / Richard W. Strong, Harvey F. Silver, Matthew J. Perini.
        p. cm.
Includes bibliographical references (p.) and index.
    ISBN 0-87120-518-1 (alk. paper)
    1. Thought and thinking—Study and teaching—United States. 2. Education—Standards—United States. I. Silver, Harvey F. II. Perini, Matthew J., 1973– III. Title.
    LB1590.3 .S52 2001
    379.1'58'0973—dc21
                                                    2001003384

07 06 05 04 03 02   10 9 8 7 6 5 4 3 2

Dedication

ABRAHAM LINCOLN REMINDED US AT GETTYSBURG about our inability to dedicate, consecrate or hallow the ground on which we stand. The implication is that someone braver has always gone before us. In our case it is no different, though the ground we walk upon was created by teachers. Some of these, Ann Brown, Magdalene Lampert, Deborah Ball, Ellin Keene, Susan Zimmermann, Phyllis and David Whitin, are teacher-researchers whom we know only from books and articles. Their bravery consists of commitment to balancing their time in lab and library, with ongoing work as teachers in U.S. classrooms. In making this commitment they have created a new kind of research more practical and more profound than any we have seen. Another group to whom we owe our deepest thanks includes several hundred full-time practicing teachers and administrators who have worked with us during the last 10 years in formulating and applying the ideas in this book. Their work is represented in this book by Claudia Geocaris, Joanne Curran, Barb Heinzman, Ed Wright, Sherry Gibbon, Carl Carrozza, John Duffy, Wende Brock, Pat Lynch, Ann Dillon, Debra Shrout, Kristen Perini, Abigail Silver, Eva Benevento, Robin Cederblad, Della Bryant, Gail Hirst, Jackie Spencer, Kay Buffamante, and Judy Ingalls. And yet it is to a third group of teachers to whom we actually dedicate this book:

To Grant Wiggins and Jay McTighe, who taught us that thinking rigorously was an act of friendship;

To Bena Kallick and Art Costa, who taught us to listen to the spirit of thought, not merely to itemize its strategies; and

To Robert Marzano and Giselle Martin-Kniep, who continue to teach us the relationship between careful and care.

None of these people, who taught us so much, have a home in either a university or a school. They live in a strange new world between the two and their courage lies in living there—permanent strangers, permanent friends. And yet they did not create this world, this strange middle ground that has proven so fruitful to researcher-teachers, teacher-researchers. This world was created by two men, Gordon Cawelti and Ron Brandt, who had their own teachers and who passed their vision on to the good care of Eugene Carter, Sally Chapman, Mikki Terry, John O'Neil, Agnes Crawford, and some 200 other employees. And let's not forget our editor and teacher, Mark Goldberg, who, like all the others, had his own teachers.

Thank you for the ground we walk upon.

Teaching What Matters Most
Standards and Strategies for Raising Student Achievement

List of Figures

Introduction

THIS IS A BOOK ABOUT RESPONSIBILITY—ABOUT OUR responsibility to teach what matters most to the increasingly diverse students who face us in our classrooms. It is a practical book, packed with the tools that can enable us to meet this responsibility. It is a positive book, filled with examples of schools, teachers, and administrators around the country who are helping students achieve high levels of performance on state and national assessments. Finally, this book is based on the simple premise that these goals can be achieved by putting in place three simple, but deep, changes in the practice of schooling. We call these changes responsible standards, responsible strategies, and responsible assessment practices, because the three taken together make it possible for schools to fulfill their responsibilities to their students. In our vision, they are what matter most in U.S. education today.

What Are Responsible Standards?

Ten years ago, near the start of the standards-based movement in education, we asked this question: *Is there a set of standards that would lead to measurable improvement on a variety of state tests, while still permitting schools and teachers the creativity they need to meet the needs of all their students?*

Working with more than 300 schools nationwide, we soon realized that the standards we were searching for needed to fit three criteria. The standards had to enable students to meet the varying standards in all 50 states, elicit popular support (to be understandable and attractive to diverse communities and constituencies across the nation), and be manageable (schools needed to feel they could help the vast majority of their students meet these standards).

Over time, four such standards emerged:

1) Rigor. All students need to be able to read and understand powerful and challenging texts and the ideas that animate them;

2) Thought. All students need to acquire the disciplines of learning: They need to be able to collect and organize information, to speak and write effectively, to master the arts of inquiry and problem solving, and to be able

to reflect on and learn from their own activity as learners.

3) Diversity. All students need to understand their own strengths and weaknesses, their unique styles, intelligences, and cultural heritages, and be able to use that knowledge to understand and work with people different from themselves.

4) Authenticity. All students need to be able to apply what they learn to settings beyond the school doors—especially those settings governed by the goals of citizenship and future careers.

As we worked with schools to implement these standards, we found that though the standards were seemingly broad, student progress toward the standards was measurable and assessable. Just as encouraging, these four standards proved to be applicable to all content areas. But we also found that these standards, while necessary to student improvement, were insufficient on their own. Responsible standards were what mattered most but they were not *all* that mattered.

What Are Responsible Strategies?

It is irresponsible to insist on new and higher standards and not provide teachers with the strategies they need to enable students to meet these standards. The strategies in this book had to meet two standards of their own:

• They had to be research-based. All the strategies in this book contain at least a 10-year research base demonstrating their effectiveness in helping students meet the standards; and,

• They had to be transferable. The strategies are not, strictly speaking, teaching strategies. Rather, they are learning strategies—strategies students can learn and apply independently to their own content area learning.

We saw early on that these criteria were essential if our standards and strategies were to

empower students to master the variety of curriculum goals described by state standards. But, as we worked with schools incorporating our new responsible standards and strategies, we realized that our vision of what mattered most led to student improvement but was still incomplete. One more factor was necessary to complete the picture.

What Are Responsible Assessment Practices?

We cannot respond to student needs without a clear picture of what those needs are and how they change over time. But what sort of assessment practices would increase teachers' and schools' abilities to respond thoughtfully? As we studied the assessment literature, three criteria for responsible assessment practices emerged:

• They are evaluative. Assessment helps us determine how close to, or how far from a given standard our students' thinking and performances are. In this way assessment is like a ladder, in that it allows us to see how well students are climbing the rungs, becoming better and more sophisticated learners and thinkers;

• They are reflective. Responsible assessment opens a window into each student's mind, helping both the teacher and student see how the student thinks and what interests, learning styles, and multiple intelligences attract the student's attention and deepen the student's understanding;

• They are supported. Most classroom assessment should take place in contexts where the teacher can coach and instruct the student, and where the student has the ability to access relevant materials and to discuss his work with other students. If we do not make regular use of supported assessment, then we will not know what strategies and types of support help the student learn best.

All of the assessment strategies included in this book meet these criteria.

So there you have it. Our answer to the question, What matters most? Responsible standards, responsible strategies, and responsible assessment practices. Tie them together and they can help us create schools that are capable of accepting and meeting their responsibilities to all our learners.

The Plan of the Book

Teaching What Matters Most is divided into four sections—one for each of the four standards—Rigor, Thought, Diversity, and Authenticity. Each section contains three chapters. The first chapter in each section introduces the standard and provides a definition in action, showing what the standard looks like in various classrooms and school settings. The second chapter in each section introduces the learning strategies that help students to meet that standard. The concluding chapter in each section maps out the assessment practices teachers can use to understand student needs as they work toward these standards. In the 13th and final chapter, we ask how a whole school can become responsible for student learning. In response, we provide three practical strategies from the lives of schools, showing how teachers and administrators have organized schools so that they are focused on the goal of teaching what matters most.

1

Standard 1: Rigor

A CERTAIN SEVERITY SURROUNDS THE CONCEPT OF rigor. We imagine detailed discussions on the fine points of grammar; endless repetition of chemical formulas; long hours of drill and practice. But this is not at all what rigor should look like. Here are some different images:

• At Agnes Irwin School in Rosemont, Pennsylvania, teacher Barbara Barnett shows her French students a videotaped interview she had conducted with Marcel Jabelot (Barnett, 1995). In the interview, conducted entirely in French, the 70-year-old Jabelot discusses his experiences in the Holocaust and his lifelong quest to find meaning in his suffering and the suffering of others. The students lean forward, their eyes focused and intent. They often stop the video to take notes, look up terms, and discuss what Jabelot is trying to tell them. As they study the video, the students' own vocabularies begin to shift. They no longer sound like the textbook. As Barnett tells it, "Their voices are full of Jabelot."

• During the 1970s, poet Kenneth Koch (1990) journeyed into the New York City public schools, reading the works of Blake, Wordsworth, Dickinson, and other poets with students from 3rd to 9th grades. Koch taught his students how to read the great poetry of Eastern and Western literature. He showed them how to extract the central struggle, the poetic kernel, from what they read and how to use those ideas to enhance their own understanding and writing. According to Koch, nearly every literature textbook written for elementary students underrates the abilities of young readers to understand and appreciate poetry.

• Students in a 5th grade classroom in Briarcliff, New York, are reading books by logician Raymond Smullyan. They study the puzzles in his book, *What Is the Name of This Book? The Riddle of Dracula and Other Logical Puzzles* (1978) and discover an "error" he has made in the definition of a formal category. The students write Smullyan a letter explaining the discovery. He writes back acknowledging the confusion and thanking them for their insights. Later in the year, these same students will study number theory, explaining their answers to questions like, "What is the largest product that can be obtained from a series of addends whose sum is given?" Over the course of the next three years, the students' scores on the New York State tests soar from seventeenth to third in the county.

• In the Humanitas Program in Los Angeles, California, the children from the poorest neighborhoods are studying the works of Hobbes, Locke, and Jefferson. They read *The Myth of Sisyphus* by Camus and Sartre's *No Exit.* They are trying to understand the relationship between liberty and power, and how different concepts of these ideas played themselves out in colonial and modern times. During our visit there, an elaborately tattooed young man stopped us in the hallway to initiate a discussion about whether people's beliefs regarding liberty are solely a function of their economic interests.

Before defining rigor, we ask you use Figure 1.1 to examine your own experiences with rigor.

As you approach the work of teaching in a rigorous manner, it is helpful to remember what rigor is *not:*

• *Rigor is not a special program or curriculum for select students.* The students in the opening vignettes are not part of programs for the gifted. Nor are they students in special magnet schools. They are ordinary students attending traditional public schools where standardized tests and state-run curricula are the rule of the day.

• *Rigor is not about severity or hardship.* The classrooms we have looked into are both warm and challenging.

• *Rigor is not about back-to-basics.* It is not an attempt to roll back education to some prior ideal state, or to find a curriculum that is some-how more fundamental or natural.

• *Rigor is not about higher-order thinking.* The examples are concerned with the content students were learning, not on how they were asked to think about it.

• *Rigor is neither a conservative nor a liberal agenda that privileges the ideas of one civilization over another.* No culture has any prior or superior claim on rigor; the students in our vignettes examined content from a rich variety of cultures.

FIGURE 1.1
REFLECTING ON YOUR IMAGES OF RIGOR

What have been some of your experiences with rigorous content as a student, and how have those experiences affected you as a teacher?

As a Student:

• What subjects or courses did you find most difficult?
• Did you ever have a teacher who taught in a rigorous manner? In what ways? How did you respond?
• Did you ever have a teacher whose expectations of you were too high?
• When you studied something demanding, what made that subject difficult? How did you go about gaining control over the content?
• Did you ever have a teacher who taught in a non-rigorous, undemanding manner? How did that affect you?
• What does all this mean to you as a teacher?

As a Teacher:

• What have been your experiences with teaching—or attempting to teach—rigorously?
• What do these experiences suggest about how you might teach in the future?
• What are some ideas or texts you have taught, or would like to teach, that you consider rigorous? Which of these do you consider too difficult for your students? What makes them so difficult? What skills would your students need to master the material?
• When you are teaching a particularly difficult idea or text, how do you go about it? How do your students respond?
• What are the chief roadblocks facing you in your attempts to increase the rigor of the content you teach?

• *Finally—and most important—rigor is not a measure of the* quantity *of content to be covered.* Rather, rigor is a measure of that content's quality.

So, What *Is* Rigor?

Now that we've settled the background—what you think about rigor and what rigor is not— here's our definition:

Rigor is the goal of helping students develop the capacity to understand content that is *complex, ambiguous, provocative, and personally or emotionally challenging.*

This definition has three characteristics that may strike some readers as peculiar:

First, the definition describes rigor as a *curriculum goal.* Most definitions define rigor simply as difficulty. By making it a goal, we are asserting that the ability to manage difficult content is a fundamental skill all students need, in school and out.

Second, the definition requires that students regularly work with difficult texts and ideas. In focusing on the role of content, we are supporting David Perkins' assertion in *Smart Schools: Better Thinking & Learning for Every Child* (1992) that the most important decision we make is not *how* to teach, but *what* to teach. In fact, the decision to withhold rigor from some students is one of the most important reasons why schools fail. All students need schools to provide both rigorous content and direct instruction in the skills needed to manage that content (e.g., note making, summarizing, glossing a text).

Third, the definition points out the different ways in which content can become rigorous.

• Some contents, like molecular biology or economics, are *complex,* composed of interacting and overlapping ideas (think cellular respiration, the structure of an ecosystem, or the causes of depressions or recessions).

• Others are *provocative,* conceptually challenging, dealing with dilemmas, engaging students in identifying problems, conducting inquiry, taking positions (think of human cloning or the themes of Richard Wright's *Native Son* or Katherine Paterson's *Bridge to Terabithia*).

• Still others, like modern poetry, primary documents, and statistics, are *ambiguous,* packed with multiple meanings that must be examined and sorted into patterns of significance (e.g., Dickinson's "The Soul Selects Her Own Society," or A. A. Milne's *The House at Pooh Corner,* or a database describing U.S. immigration patterns from 1875 to 1920).

• Finally, some content is *personally or emotionally challenging* (the novels of Toni Morrison or Lois Lowry, the facts of Shay's Rebellion, or the Trail of Tears). How might they personally challenge students and their sense of how the world works?

The diversity of ways that content can become difficult implies that using one or two strategies for instruction or assessment will not be sufficient to help students learn to manage rigor. Teachers will need a repertoire of strategies keyed to the different ways content can be difficult.

Experiencing Rigor: Get the Sensation!

Chocolate, popular food made from the beans of the cacao plant. The outer husks of the beans are stripped away through a process of fermentation and roasting that breaks the kernels into small fragments. These fragments (called nibs) are pressed to produce cocoa butter, which is then combined with sugar and sometimes milk. Chocolate is high in carbohydrates and contains caffeine. It is often sold in bars, as a powder to be used in baking, or used to create beverages.

Although that is a typical definition, you could mull over the definition for hours without knowing what chocolate really is. Quite simply, if you want to know what chocolate is, you've got to taste it. It's the same thing with rigor. To know rigor is to experience it, to "get the sensation." Figure 1.2 gives you examples of

FIGURE 1.2
EXAMPLES OF DIFFICULT IDEAS

In *The House at Pooh Corner*, A. A. Milne describes the difference between young streams and old rivers:

BY THE TIME it came to the edge of the Forest, the stream had grown up, so that it was almost a river, and, being grown-up, it did not run and jump and sparkle along as it used to do when it was younger, but moved more slowly. For it knew now where it was going, and it said to itself, "There is no hurry. We shall get there some day." But all the little streams higher up in the Forest went this way and that, quickly, eagerly, having so much to find out before it was too late.

"Pooh Invents a New Game and Eeyore Joins in" from *The House at Pooh Corner* by A. A. Milne, Illustrations by E. H. Shepard, copyright 1928 by E. P. Dutton. Renewed copyright 1956 by A. A. Milne. Used by permission of Dutton Children's Books, a division of Penguin Putnam Inc.

Henry David Thoreau discusses the proper role of government in *Civil Disobedience*:

I HEARTILY accept the motto, "That government is best which governs least"; and I should like to see it acted up to more rapidly and systematically. Carried out, it finally amounts to this, which also I believe—"That government is best which governs not at all"; and when men are prepared for it, that will be the kind of government which they will have. Government is at best but an expedient; but most governments are usually, and all governments are sometimes, inexpedient. The objections which have been brought against a standing army, and they are many and weighty, and deserve to prevail, may also at last be brought against a standing government. The standing army is only an arm of the standing government. The government itself, which is only the mode which the people have chosen to execute their will, is equally liable to be abused and perverted before the people can act through it. Witness the present Mexican war, the work of comparatively a few individuals using the standing government as their tool; for, in the outset, the people would not have consented to this measure.

"Civil Disobedience" from *Walden, or Life in the Woods and Other Writings*, 1937/1993, New York: Barnes and Noble Books.

W. E. B. Du Bois reveals his experience of being black in a world of whites in *The Souls of Black Folk*:

BETWEEN me and the other world there is ever an unasked question: unasked by some through feelings of delicacy; by others through the difficulty of rightly framing it. All, nevertheless, flutter round it. They approach me in a half-hesitant sort of way, eye me curiously or compassionately, and then, instead of saying directly, How does it feel to be a problem? they say, I know an excellent colored man in my town; or, I fought at Mechanicsville; or, Do not these Southern outrages make your blood boil? At these I smile, or am interested, or reduce the boiling to a simmer, as the occasion may require. To the real question, How does it feel to be a problem? I answer seldom a word.

From *The Souls of Black Folk*, W. E. B. Du Bois 1989, New York: Bantam Classics

Emily Dickinson reflects on the process of decision making in "The Soul Selects Her Own Society":

> The Soul selects her own Society—
> Then—shuts the Door—
> To her divine Majority—
> Present no more—
>
> Unmoved—she notes the Chariots—pausing—
> At her low Gate—
> Unmoved—an Emperor be kneeling
> Upon her Mat—
>
> I've known her—from an ample nation—
> Choose One—
> Then—close the Valves of her attention—
> Like Stone—

"The Soul Selects Her Own Society" from *Collected Poems of Emily Dickinson*, 1986, New York: Avenel Books.

In a math textbook, the authors describe how Carl Friedrich Gauss, at the age of 10, added up all the counting numbers from 1 to 100 in a matter of seconds:

To find the requested sum $(1 + 2 + 3 + 4 + 5 + ?+ 97 + 98 + 99 + 100)$, Gauss noticed that when the first and last terms were added, the sum was 101. Likewise, when the second and next-to-last terms were added, the sum was 101, as it was when the third and the third-from-last terms were added, and so on. Since Gauss knew that the order in which the numbers were added did not matter, he recognized that the problem could be solved by adding up pairs, each of which added to 101. That is,

$$(1 + 2 + 3 + 4 + 5 + \ldots + 97 + 98 + 99 + 100) =$$
$$(1 + 100) + (2 + 99) + (3 + 98) + \ldots + (50 + 51)$$

And how many *pairs* were there? Fifty. So the sum must be 50 x 101, or 5050.

From *Patterns in Mathematics Problem Solving from Counting to Chaos 1st ed.*, 1994, Pacific Grove, CA: Thomson Learning. Copyright 1994 by Michael Sequeira. Reprinted with permission.

rigorous content to sample. We couldn't insert *Moby Dick,* so we selected some descriptions of difficult ideas from a variety of content areas. Browse through them. Then select one or two to concentrate on and make a sincere effort to understand what their authors are trying to say. Enjoy! Get the sensation!

What Does Rigor Mean and Why Does It Matter?

We hope you found our rigorous samples more like a wine-tasting than an algebra test. The key is that all kinds of rigors are not the same. Some, like the explanation of how Gauss solved problems, are difficult because they are *complex*—made up of intricate and interrelated ideas. Others, like the excerpt from Thoreau's "Civil Disobedience," are *provocative*—they challenge our natural ways of thinking and believing. Still others, like Dickinson's poem, are *ambiguous*—rich in symbols, images, and multiple meanings. Here the sample from Milne's *The House at Pooh Corner* is notable because, unlike most children's literature, its content is metaphorical as well as descriptive. Finally, some content is *emotionally or personally challenging*—it arouses strong or unfamiliar feelings, as does W. E. B. Du Bois's picture of black people at the turn of the century.

Interacting with and working their way through difficult texts in all four types is essential if students are to grow as learners. In making this claim, we affirm the idea that content *is* important. Yet by narrowing attention too closely on individual bits of information, or by emphasizing only generalized themes, the educational community has in many ways lost sight of deep, rich, and substantive content.

Regular use of rigorous texts and content at all grade levels is important for five reasons:

1. Rigorous reading and content demand attention. Simplistic textbooks and content that has been "dumbed down," require little thought or attention, they do little to help students enhance their capacities in either attention or critical thinking. On the other hand, Thoreau's "Civil Disobedience" or the explanation of how Gauss solved a difficult math problem (see Figure 1.2) compel our attention. We know from the outset that understanding these will not be easy. A wind blows across our face and we awaken.

2. Rigorous reading and content help us to handle uncertainty. Simplistic texts and ideas seduce us with seeming clarity. They hide complexities and obscure interrelationships. But when we read Emily Dickinson's "The Soul Selects Her Own Society," our minds come alive with questions: Why does she use the word *society*? What does she mean by *chariots* and the *emperor*? What is the *ample nation*? When we succeed in making sense of passages like these, we have new resources for handling uncertainty, not only in texts but in our lives.

3. Rigorous content increases flexibility in thinking. Making sense of difficult material teaches us to follow a train of thought, to come to terms with nuance and subtlety. With practice, we build complex intellectual schema that are broad, flexible, and adaptable to a rich variety of situations. Very simple schema ("survival of the fittest," stereotypes, "I don't know much about art, but I know what I like") can easily become the unexamined core of thought and action. Students raised on bland and featureless texts and ideas are thus left without the resources they need to handle academic learning, or the surprises of a constantly changing world.

Take another look at Du Bois's introduction to *The Souls of Black Folk* (Figure 1.2). Notice how the author's delay in asking the crucial question forces the reader to contemplate the context in which the question fails to appear, and to experience the awkwardness of the white speakers and its effect on the black listener. This is exactly the kind of emotional and contextual complexity that supports the creation of flexible schema in the minds of readers and learners.

4. *Rigor develops perseverance, intellectual modesty, and tolerance.* Rigorous material rewards effort. The more we think about a rigorous text or concept, the deeper our thoughts become and the more we discover about the conditions of our own lives. The difficulties we confront remind us how hard it is to fully understand the positions of others, and how likely we are to misunderstand their ideas by imposing our own understanding on them. In this way rigor develops not just cognitive understanding but character as well, teaching us to persevere when meaning is not obvious, and to respect the complexity and rationality of others' thoughts.

5. *Rigor creates self-confidence.* How many of our students feel condescended to by the texts and ideas that comprise their curriculum? How much secret condescension underlies the idea that the next activity will be fun or easy? How much better is it to tell students that these ideas are difficult, that they will challenge their intellect? If they succeed, they will bring new confidence to the next task; if they temporarily fail, they will retain pride because the challenge they faced was a worthy one.

Here we have failed to learn from coaches. Coaches rarely say, "This is going to be easy," because they know the pride and self-respect of their players depend on confronting challenges. A coach who says, "This is going to be hard," is really saying, "This will be an adventure worthy of your attention, energy, and perseverance. I present you with this challenge because I believe in you. If I thought less of you, I would give you a smaller challenge."

With these ideas in mind, we can begin to ask ourselves questions about the curriculum we teach in our schools.

Reflecting and Discussing

Figure 1.3 is a chart for measuring and discussing the rigor in your school or classroom as a prelude to informed discussion. Rate your curriculum on a scale of one, the least, to four, the most. What signs and what indicators in your content support this rating? What would need to happen to increase the rigor in your curriculum?

Quick Tips for Increasing Rigor in Your Classroom

Elementary

• *Make Room for Pooh!* Increase the role of chapter books at read-aloud time in the primary grades.

• *Bite Off More Than You Can Chew!* Announce today that your 5th graders will be performing *A Midsummer Night's Dream* this spring.

• *Rigorous Mondays.* Set aside 30 minutes each week to read classical and contemporary rigorous texts to your students. Why wait for middle school or high school for *Jane Eyre* or *Emma*? Eleanor Roosevelt didn't!

• *Use the "Measuring Rigor Scale."* Evaluate your textbooks, classroom, and school libraries against Figure 1.3. What kinds of rigor are you lacking? Have you looked into the *Touchpebbles Program,* examined the *Junior Great Books Textbook Series,* or contemplated the *Comprehensive School Mathematics Program*? All of these score high on the rigor scale.

• *Read Together.* Set up reading groups for the adults in your school. Don't read children's literature. Read adult literature, and talk about it. Why not start with Sandra Cisneros's *House on Mango Street,* or Edward Ball's *Slaves in the Family,* or Shakespeare's *The Tempest*?

Secondary

• *Increase the Use of Primary Documents.* History has a history, and so do science and math.

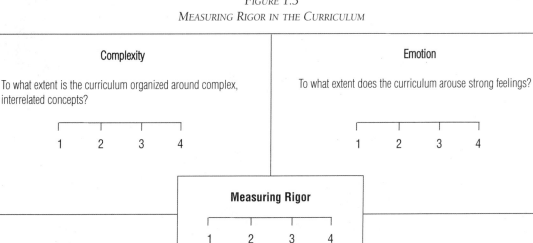

FIGURE 1.3
MEASURING RIGOR IN THE CURRICULUM

Complexity

To what extent is the curriculum organized around complex, interrelated concepts?

1   2   3   4

Emotion

To what extent does the curriculum arouse strong feelings?

1   2   3   4

Measuring Rigor

1   2   3   4

Provocativeness

To what extent is the curriculum concerned with central problems in the discipline that challenge students' previous concepts?

1   2   3   4

Ambiguity

To what extent does the curriculum focus on symbols and images packed with multiple meanings?

1   2   3   4

Not studying and reading this history is a nearly perfect demonstration of a lack of rigor.

• *Rigorous Tuesdays.* Set aside 30 to 45 minutes each week to read aloud or to read with all your students examples of challenging and rigorous texts. Why wait for college to provide students with excerpts from Darwin's *The Origin of Species*?

• *Read Math!* Take a serious look at textbooks like the *Connected Math Series* (Lappan, Fey, Fitzgerald, Friel, & Phillips, 1998) and the *University of Chicago School Mathematics Project* that are sophisticated mathematically, with substantive readings on math concepts.

• *Get Philosophical!* Add philosophy texts to all courses, or create new philosophy-oriented courses from middle through high school. For example, how about making *The Philosophy of Human Rights* (Winston, 1989) the frame for current events or history classes? Or, how about World Literature classes that look at Harold Bloom's *The Western Canon* as a way of thinking about how cultures decide which texts are important? Why not use John Horgan's controversial *The End of Science* to explore the concept of limits to knowledge in science classes? Or, *Thinking Mathematically* (Mason, Burton, Stacey, 1985) in math? The possibilities are both endless and provocative.

• *Diversify Your Texts.* Secondary school textbooks are usually too broad and shallow to be rigorous. Systematically collect articles and books that discuss aspects of your content provocatively. Last year 100 new math titles and 150 new science titles passed through our corner bookstore. Why aren't more of these titles in our schools?

    • *A Department Is a Club for Readers.* Ask the members of department, whether it's science, social studies, history, English, math, foreign language, art, or physical education, to read a book together and discuss it. Better still, read different books and make presentations to each other. One rule: No books on pedagogy allowed!

Strategies for Rigorous Learning

TWO YEARS AGO DEBRA SHROUT, A HIGH SCHOOL English teacher and department chair in Kirkwood High School, Kirkwood, Missouri, was leading a double life: In the morning she taught "high-interest" adolescent literature to low-achieving 9th graders. In the afternoon she read *The Iliad* with some of the school's highest achievers. Debra explained:

> After a while, I couldn't take the division any more—knowing I was giving half my students a first-rate education, while the other half was getting less—something smaller, diminished somehow. It occurred to me that it might be interesting to read something stronger with my morning classes. In a workshop we had a few months ago on raising standards, we read a few chapters of Charles Dickens' *Hard Times.* We could use *Hard Times,* I thought, to examine the process of education, something central to all students' lives. We could organize the reading around a simple but essential question: "What makes a good education?"

Debra went back to the notes she had taken at the workshop. The first part of *Hard Times* she had been asked to respond to at the workshop introduced the character Stephen Blackpool. Debra's notes read like this:

At first I felt totally lost. There seemed to be so much coming at me. I felt irritated. Why is he writing this way? I thought it might be vocabulary, but when I looked back, none of the words were particularly difficult. So I slowed down and noticed that the reading was broken up into sections. Each section began with a preposition, so I marked the passage up.

To understand how Debra began to methodically examine the passage, see Figure 2.1.

Approaching the task in this manner gave her insight:

> Now I could see how the passage was put together. Each of the parts was trying to tell me where Stephen Blackpool came from. In the margin I jotted down words and ideas that struck me as important. When I looked back, I saw that Dickens wanted me to see that Stephen came from a terrible place where he was cut off from nature, gassed, polluted, jammed in against everyone else, and forced there by someone—industrialists maybe—who only wanted him to work and eat. So then I asked myself why Dickens wrote the passage this way, in one long sentence. Maybe he wanted me to feel like Stephen: lost in all

FIGURE 2.1
DEBRA'S MARKED PASSAGE

<u>In the hardest working part</u> of Coketown; <u>in the inner-most fortifications</u> of that ugly citadel, where Nature was as strongly bricked out as killing airs and gasses were bricked in; <u>at the heart of the labyrinth</u> of narrow courts upon courts, and close streets upon streets, which had come into existence piecemeal, every piece in a violent hurry for some one man's purpose, and the whole an unnatural family, shouldering, and trampling, and pressing one another to death; <u>in the last close nook of this great exhausted receiver</u>, where the chimneys, for want of air to make a draught, were built in an immense variety of stunted and crooked shapes, as though every house put out a sign of the kind of people who might be expected to be born in it; <u>among the multitude of Coketown</u>, generically called "the Hands"—a race who could have found more favour with some people if Providence had seen fit to make them only hands, or, like the lower creatures of the seashore, only hands and stomachs—lived a certain Stephen Blackpool, forty years of age.	no nature gasses narrow violent hurry unnatural trampling crammed together stunted and crooked shapes only hands and stomachs

Source: Text from *Hard Times* by C. Dickens (1854/1991)

these words like Stephen was lost in this awful place.

Debra is an excellent reader. But before we credit her success solely to her innate abilities and throw up our hands with a chorus of "Our kids can't do this!", let's look at the moves Debra made:

• She paid attention to her own reading process (*metacognition*).

• She marked the text and took notes in the margins (*glossing*).

• She searched for patterns that could help her find a structure in what she was reading (*structuring*).

• She consciously thought out an image of the text's meaning (*image making*).

• She summarized her understanding as she went along (*retelling*).

• She raised questions for clarification to deepen her understanding (*questioning*).

• She compared what she was reading with her personal experience and knowledge (*making connections*).

• She discovered a purpose for reading (*seeking purpose*).

Each move Debra made corresponds to learning skills that researchers have found to be prominent among expert readers and absent among novice readers (e.g., Keene and Zimmerman's *Mosaic of Thought*, 1997); each skill has been shown to improve the quality of student learning when modeled and practiced. Unfortunately, less than 15 percent of classroom time is spent modeling the skills students need most to make sense of challenging content. Students must either acquire these skills on their own or fail to learn how to work through rigorous material. Because so many students lack these skills, many teachers reduce the rigor of the content taught and the texts assigned, setting off a downward spiral that is gradually driving rigor out of the U.S. school curriculum.

There is another way. Not only can these skills be modeled, practiced, and discussed regularly, but by using instructional strategies that facilitate the development of these skills, teachers can create dynamic classrooms that motivate students to become rigorous learners.

Strategies for Managing Rigorous Content

How do you introduce rigorous content to your students, some of whom have never been challenged in this way? The following strategies can ease the transition for both students and teachers.

Split-Screen Notes

Claudia Geocaris of Hinsdale South High School in Illinois is about to teach her sophomore biology class an important lesson about the body's circulatory system. She begins this way:

> Here's an interesting problem in biology. Imagine a typical toy train set. Little tracks running around in a circle. Tiny stations along the way. An engine and a couple of cars. Now, imagine it filled with toy cargo—plastic cows, barrels of grain. All the tracks are encased in a tunnel. Do you see any problem here?

Student: You can't see the trains.

Student: No way to unload the cargo.

> Right, good. Now, do you see this is a little like our circulatory system? The blood running in the blood vessels, needing to unload nutrients and on-load waste products for all the cells. But it's blind. How does it know how to off-load the nutrients and on-load the waste products, without getting them mixed up? Now, that's a biological question, and the man who figured out how the body solved this problem was an Englishman named Ernest Starling. We're going to examine his solution today. At the same time, we're going

to explore an important issue in scientific learning—using diagrams to clarify our pictures of how the body works.

Claudia passes out a simple worksheet divided into two parts: the left side labeled "words," the right, "diagram."

> Here's how it's going to go. I'm going to read you a passage that describes Starling's Solution. I'm going to read it twice. The first time, use the left side of your paper to jot down clues to how this works. The second time I read it, use the clues and what you're hearing to construct a diagram that shows how the circulatory system dispenses nutrients and collects waste products in the capillaries.

As Claudia reads, the students take notes and construct their diagrams. Then in small teams they compare their diagrams, discussing discrepancies. Next, they examine the diagram in the textbook. Claudia closes this part of the lesson with a discussion on the role diagrams play in communicating and learning about science. See Figure 2.2 for an example of the notes taken by the students during the exercise.

In this episode, Claudia is employing a strategy called Split-Screen Notes. The strategy moves through five steps:

1. The teacher selects a dense or rigorous passage and reads it aloud twice to the class.
2. While the teacher reads the passage the first time, either students create sketches or diagrams to represent the information they are hearing, or they take notes on which to base later sketches or diagrams.
3. During the second reading, students either take notes or draw a diagram, whichever they did not do during the first reading.
4. Then they meet in small groups to compare their work and discuss differences in their notes and drawings.

FIGURE 2.2
SPLIT-SCREEN NOTES

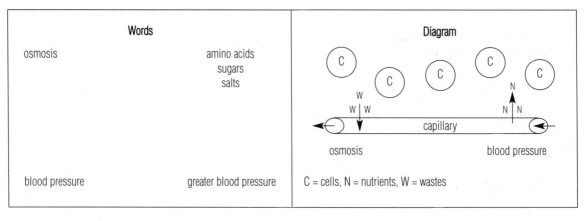

5. Over time, students learn how to use both the visual and the verbal elements in their notebooks independently.

Claudia explained to us why she chose this process to teach a difficult concept:

> I read somewhere there are twice as many new words in a biology text as there are in the first *two* years of a foreign language. For the kids I teach, this is very tough stuff. They open their textbooks, and all they see is a great wave of words coming at them. They need some way of sorting through all that strange and awkward language. That's why I begin by setting a purpose—establishing a biological problem or question to act as a lens—in this case, one called Split-Screen Notes—that combines note taking, sketching, and discussion, because I want them every day to be not just learning science, but learning how to learn. Some of my friends don't agree with me. They say it's not their job to teach reading, but what am I supposed to do? The kids I teach need both.

Claudia recognizes the kind of rigor (complexity) embedded in the content she's teaching. She understands that the problem with complex texts and ideas is that they may overwhelm learners. But she also understands that providing students with an organizer would, in fact, disable them—she would miss an opportunity to teach them how to handle complexity on their own. For this reason, Claudia uses a problem-based *purpose* (how does the circulatory system dispense its nutrients?) and a particular strategy (Split-Screen Notes) to help students *structure* and *make images* of the complexity they are dealing with.

Glossing

Eight students meet for two hours with Debra Shrout for a combination English and Social Studies class. All Debra's students are in special education, with reading levels between 6th and 8th grade. Debra feels comfortable here: she believes reading is problem-solving, and her students know they have a problem with reading. Although many special education teachers rely on programmed instruction, Debra teaches her students how to handle the most difficult texts imaginable. Today, they will be reading from W. E. B. Du Bois's *Souls of Black Folk*.

Debra begins by having students take a few minutes to read the opening paragraph. She shows them how to divide a notebook page into two vertical halves, the left one headed "Response" and the right one headed "Text."

Under "Response," students record their responses, which may be questions, thoughts, reactions, or connections. On the right side, they jot down what in the text provoked their responses.

As the students read and write, Debra moves around the room, sitting down next to students and asking them how they're doing. Some are puzzled, others dazed. Most, at least, are dutifully involved. After a few minutes Debra asks them to do a quick "buddy up," to share their reactions with another student and look for responses they had in common. She calls the class together after just two or three minutes and asks if she can collect and record some of their responses on the board. After a few minutes, the board looks like Figure 2.3.

Debra then leads the class in discussion.

Debra: What do you notice?

Student: Lots of questions—not many thoughts or reactions—we're not getting it.

Debra: We've been here before. What do you suppose is the problem? Ours—not the writer's, right?

Student: Well, he goes on and we don't know what he's talking about.

Debra: I had trouble with it at first, too. Later on, I learned to love it, but first I had to work it through. So, since there are so many questions, let's suppose for a minute that the problem is that we can't yet see the structure of what he's saying and why he's saying it in this complicated way. Here's a way we can hunt this out: Let's mark up the text a bit. [Debra places a transparency of the text on the overhead.] Let's place a question mark over "other

FIGURE 2.3
WHAT DOES IT MEAN TO BE A PROBLEM?

What does it mean to be a problem?

What's "the other world," an "X File?"

Why doesn't he say what the unasked question is?

He does

Mechanicsville?

I don't like the phrase "colored people"— it's too old timey.

Where?

I don't get it.

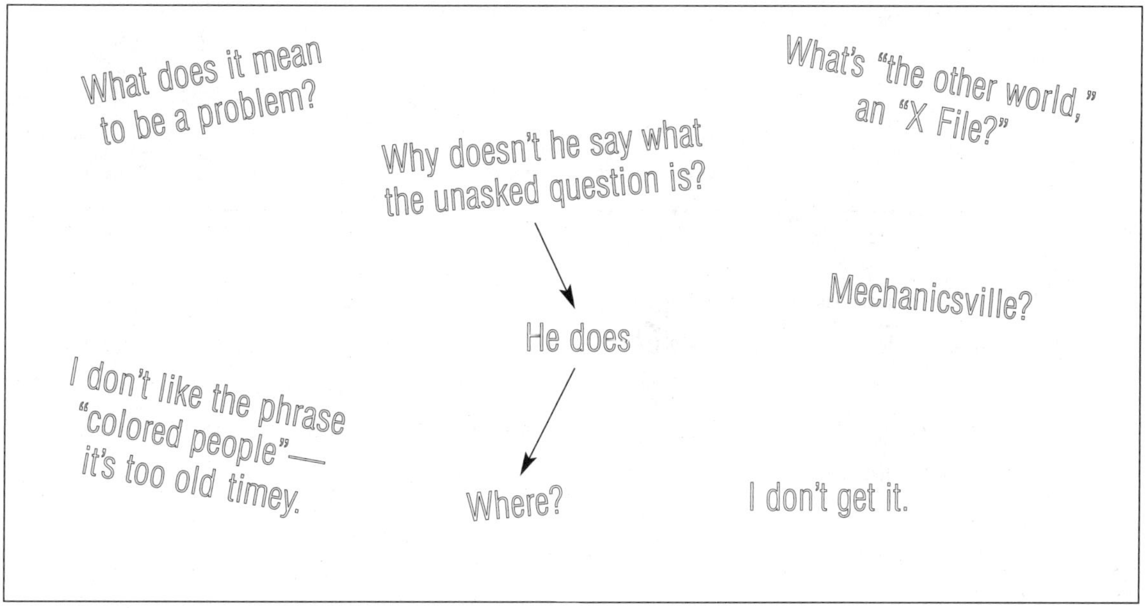

world," another over "unasked question," and another over "Mechanicsville," because we don't know what they refer to. Now, let's go on a hunt. Here's a pattern I noticed the first time I read it: See in the second line the word, "by"? And again in the third line, do you see "by" again? I'll circle them and the words that come right after them: "by some," "by others." What's going on here? Read the first four lines slowly. Stop at "framing it." See if you can figure it out with these two "bys."

Student: He's telling us why they're not asking it—the unasked question.

Debra: Great! Now let's draw two arrows from our "bys" up to ask or unask. It's about what they're not doing.

Student: Why aren't they asking the question?

Student: What *is* the question?

Debra: Good questions. [She writes them on the board and circles them.] Let's take the second question first. Read down the next few lines and see if you can spot the question.

Student: Got it. "How does it feel to be a problem?"

Debra: Excellent! Draw a circle around that. Now, what does it point to?

Student: "Unasked question."

Debra: Draw the arrow. Now, let's step back because we've got two great questions. One is yours and one is Du Bois's. Your question is, "Why aren't these people asking the question they want to ask?" Du Bois's question is, "How does it feel to be a problem?"(See Figure 2.4.)

As the class goes on, students continue working through the text, inventing and using marks other than circles, arrows, and question marks to indicate clues in the text that would help them find the answers to both the questions. Near the end of the class, Debra assigns two pieces of homework: Write your own version of the opening paragraph (*retelling*) and use the marking system the class has developed on the next section (*glossing*) to answer this question: "How are you similar to and how are you different from Du Bois? In what ways are you, too, a problem to other people?"

Debra understands that this passage is difficult for several reasons: its meaning is ambiguous,

FIGURE 2.4
MARKING TEXT FOR UNDERSTANDING

BETWEEN me and the other world there is ever an unasked question: unasked by some through feelings of delicacy; by others through the difficulty of rightly framing it. All, nevertheless, flutter around it. They approach me in a half-hesitant sort of way, eye me curiously or compassionately, and then, instead of saying directly, How does it feel to be a problem? they say, I know an excellent colored man in my town; or, I fought at Mechanicsville; or, Do not these Southern outrages make your blood boil? At these I smile, or am interested, or reduce the boiling to a simmer, as the occasion may require. To the real question, How does it feel to be a problem? I answer seldom a word.

Text Source: Du Bois (1989); copyright © Bantam Classics.

and it is both provocative and personally challenging because it explores the issue of racism with an eye toward its inner experience. Moreover, Debra identified the key problem students were having with reading it: they were not able to see the structure of what Du Bois was saying. Debra tapped into several skills essential for students trying to manage this rigorous text. She helped them recognize that they were experiencing difficulty (*metacognition*), and allowed them to talk through their responses—both in small groups and with the teacher. Debra showed students how to mark a text (*glossing*). Through this strategy, they began to identify textual patterns (*structuring*). Along the way, Debra used both her own and the students' questions to guide the process (*questioning*) and, as part of the students' homework, she asked them to summarize the reading (*retelling*) and to compare and contrast themselves with DuBois (*making connections*).

Do You See What I See?

Kristen Perini, a 5th grade teacher in Teaneck, New Jersey, was concerned with her students' achievement in math. Kristen noted that her students were not able to solve the types of complex problems found in her state's new standards and achievement tests, or to engage in authentic math-related problems. For example, here is a type of math task on the achievement tests:

> A local pizza shop offers its customers five topping choices, which they can order on top of a plain pizza: peppers, olives, mushrooms, sausage, and anchovies. Customers can order no toppings (plain), all five toppings, or any combination of toppings. How many different kinds of pizza can a customer order?

After a diagnostic period, Kristen determined that a common block to her students' achievement was not forgetting their multiplication facts, but rather that students were impulsive when it came to defining the problem and forming a solution. Before thinking about what a problem was asking, most of the students began trying to solve it. Kristen realized that rather than trying to speed students up, she would have to slow them down so that they could digest and internalize the problem, defining what it was asking and how it could best be solved.

Kristen decided to use a strategy called Do You See What I See? to slow down her students' problem-solving process. The strategy moves through these steps:

• Each week, one class period is devoted to exploring complex and nonroutine problems connected with current or past math topics (Kristen calls it Problem-Solving Friday).

• The teacher reads a problem aloud twice to the students.

• During the first reading, students take notes on the relevant information.

• During the second reading, students create a sketch representing the problem using numbers or letters (but no words) where appropriate.

• Students are provided with a written description of the problem and are asked to revise their notes—*but not to solve the problem.*

• In collaborative groups of three or four, students share their information, decide what the problem is asking for, and design a plan to solve the problem (but they still do not solve it yet).

• As the students work, the teacher circulates, observing their approaches. She asks questions, but does not provide answers or even hints. Finally, the teacher selects two or three students with different approaches to lay out their plans for the class to critique.

• For homework students are asked to solve the problem, submitting a written justification for their approach. Students do three problems like this a month, then select their best effort, meet in a response group, and revise and publish their work. The teacher grades only the published piece.

Kristen's students soon began to reformulate their relationship to mathematical problem solving. As a result, most were no longer plunging into problems without thinking about them—instead, they learned the value of a strategic plan, not just for problems used in conjunction with Do You See What I See? but in a variety of complex situations.

For Kristen, Do You See What I See? inculcated in students the following interpretive and problem-solving skills:

- *Metacognition*–Students were asked to recognize the issue: they were impulsive in defining and solving problems.
- *Glossing*–Students listened to and took notes on the problem.
- *Image Making*–Students used visualizations to represent the problem.
- *Questioning*–While circulating, the teacher probed students' understanding with questions.

Statements

In preparing her 1st-grade students for listening and reading tasks on her state's test, K–3 Special Services teacher Joanne Curran of Ladue, Missouri, regularly reads aloud to her students. This week, she is reading and discussing a story from the collection *Little Bear* by Else Homelund Minarik. In talking with her students about the story, Joanne noticed the following details:

- Although Mother Bear makes Little Bear a hat, some students missed the hat entirely.
- Most students loved Mother Bear, yet none noticed or mentioned the fact that she becomes annoyed with Little Bear.
- Every student assumed Little Bear was cold.

Joanne might have stopped at this point. After all, the students loved the story and asked to hear more. Several students sought out other *Little Bear* books to read on their own. What more could a teacher want? But it occurred to Joanne that her students hadn't *heard* the story. How could they miss the growing signs of Mother Bear's frustration? Why had some missed the hat? And why did they all assume Little Bear was cold—even though the story never says so? She knew the students had listened—after all, most could recall specific details—but, had they *understood* the story?

As Joanne saw it, the problem was one of focus: the students hadn't listened closely enough to pick up on the inferences and possibilities inherent in the story. If they were to actually hear what was going on, they needed something that would focus their attention—tune their ears—to the possible, not merely the actual.

Joanne decided to return to the story using a variation of Harold Herber's Statement Strategy (Herber, 1970; Silver, Hanson, Strong, & Schwartz, 1996) as a focusing tool. In this strategy, students are given a short set of statements about a text before they read or reread it. Statements are selected to reflect difficulties in the text. Joanne, for example, developed these statements for her class:

- Little Bear's mother made him a hat.
- Little Bear's mother thought he was a pain in the neck.
- Little Bear was cold.

Students are then asked to read (or in this case listen to) the text and search for evidence to support—or refute—the statements. They then discuss their findings first in small groups and then as a whole class, either to resolve differences or to rewrite the statements to reflect their emerging understanding of the text. Joanne selected her statements to reflect the three difficulties she had observed in her students' understanding.

FIGURE 2.5
SHAKESPEARE AND THE STATEMENT STRATEGY

FIGURE 2.5
SHAKESPEARE AND THE STATEMENT STRATEGY

Sonnet 73

That time of year thou mayst in me behold
When yellow leaves, or none, or few, do hang
Upon those boughs which shake against the cold,
Bare ruinéd choirs, where late the sweet birds sang.
In me thou see'st the twilight of such day
As after sunset fadeth in the west;
Which by and by black night doth take away,
Death's second self, that seals up all in rest.
In me thou see'st the glowing of such fire
That on the ashes of his youth doth lie
As the death-bed whereon it must expire,
Consumed with that which it was nourish'd by.
    This thou perceivést, which makes thy love more strong,
    To love that well which thou must leave ere long.

—*William Shakespeare*
from *The Sonnets of William Shakespeare* (1961)

1. The poet is a young man.   Agree   Disagree
Support for your idea.

2. This poem is mostly about nature   Agree   Disagree
Support for your idea.

3. The poet is consoling someone
   at the end of the poem.   Agree   Disagree
Support for your idea.

4. There is a connection between
   love and death in this poem.   Agree   Disagree
Support for your idea.

She also began to apply the Statement Strategy with other books she was reading to the children. At first, she used it a few times a month. As the students became comfortable with the strategy, Joanne began to use interpretive as well as literal statements. Several times she gave independent readers statements about books they had read and asked them to use the statements in describing why they liked their books, or what the characters were like.

The Statement Strategy can be used with students in any grade. Figure 2.5 shows how a high school English teacher used the strategy with 10th graders who were having difficulty reading poetry. Notice how the statements work to bring your attention to different parts of the text.

A middle-school science teacher uses the Statement Strategy for difficult passages in the text but—what's more—he often gives statements in the form of possible conclusions for labs they are about to perform. He asks students to collect evidence for and against these possible conclusions as they perform the lab (see Figure 2.6). Sometimes he gives students

FIGURE 2.6
SCIENCE AND THE STATEMENT STRATEGY

Lab Statements

As you and your partner work through this lab, collect evidence for and against the following conclusions. Which ones do the data support?

1. Gravity is the one force that is with us every second.

2. The mass of objects has nothing to do with their gravitational force.

3. Gravitational force gets stronger as you get closer to an object.

4. If the mass of one of two attracting masses is tripled, the gravitational force is tripled.

---

data collected by professional scientists along with possible conclusions and asks them to explore which conclusions the data support.

An elementary math teacher uses the Statement Strategy to help his students become more adept at analyzing word problems (Figure 2.7). To do this, he creates collaborative learning groups; together his students read the statements, determine their responses, discuss their ideas, and resolve their differences.

A global history teacher precedes all of her lectures with a set of statements that students use to examine the content of her lectures, attempting to prove or disprove the conclusions she gives them (see Figure 2.8).

FIGURE 2.7
MATH AND THE STATEMENT STRATEGY

Read the statements below. Before solving the problem, determine whether you agree or disagree, and why. As a group, discuss your answers and resolve your differences, then solve the problem.

Mr. Smith checked his cash register at the end of the day. He found that he had seven fewer $5 bills than $1 bills and no larger bills. In all, he had $327.00. Find the number of $5 and $1 bills.

1. Mr. Smith had more $5 bills than $1 bills.　　Agree　Disagree

2. The problem is asking you to find the total number of $1 bills and $5 bills.　　Agree　Disagree

3. To get this answer, you must do more than one operation.　　Agree　Disagree

4. We already know Mr. Smith's total register receipts for the day.　　Agree　Disagree

FIGURE 2.8
STATEMENTS ABOUT GENGHIS KHAN

1. Genghis Khan conquered more than half the known world.

Evidence For　　Evidence Against

2. The Chinese made several key mistakes in dealing with Genghis Khan's threat.

Evidence For　　Evidence Against

3. Genghis Khan was able to move west because Khan's soldiers were vastly superior to Europeans as fighters and as horsemen.

Evidence For　　Evidence Against

4. Genghis Khan's feats were more impressive than Alexander the Great's.

Evidence For　　Evidence Against

5. Genghis Khan has been greatly misrepresented by popular culture.

Evidence For　　Evidence Against

The point is not that the Statement Strategy is wonderful. The key is that teachers use this strategy to solve specific problems that students have in handling rigorous content. Joanne Curran uses it to help her students learn to listen deeply and make inferences; a science teacher uses it to help students navigate their way through the possibilities opened up by the large amounts of data generated in their labs; a high school English teacher uses it to help students handle ambiguous poetry; an elementary math teacher uses it to help students think through mathematical problem solving; and a global history teacher employs the strategy to help students formulate opinions and conclusions about history. How might you use it with your own students?

3 Assessing Rigor

IN TEANECK, NEW JERSEY, 6TH GRADERS ARE reading Chekhov this morning. For the past three Mondays they have met to listen to, discuss, and write about his stories. Teacher Eva Benevento begins each Monday class by reading aloud one great short story. This morning it's about a governess and an employer settling accounts. As she reads, the students take notes. Some sketch, some fill up the page with words. Several have drawn an organizer into their notebooks that looks like Figure 3.1.

One girl has already noticed that the story is essentially a dialogue between an employer and a governess and has divided her paper in half: on the left side she busily records what the employer says, while on the right she records the governess's responses. On the blackboard behind Eva hangs the poster shown in Figure 3.2.

FIGURE 3.1
ORGANIZING NOTES

Facts	Feelings
Questions	Ideas

FIGURE 3.2
WHAT MAKES A GOOD SET OF NOTES

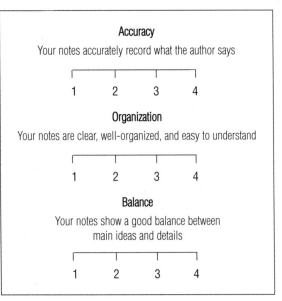

Accuracy
Your notes accurately record what the author says

1   2   3   4

Organization
Your notes are clear, well-organized, and easy to understand

1   2   3   4

Balance
Your notes show a good balance between
main ideas and details

1   2   3   4

Eva explained to us what's happening in the class:

> During September I focus on notetaking. Lots of people think I'm crazy to do this, but I don't think you're going to really think about what's going on in literature until you know the writing on a literal level. Also, I want my students to have a record of their learning. I want them to be able to revisit the works we've read and discussed throughout the year. So on Mondays throughout September I teach them five or six different notetaking techniques. But I don't have to do this alone because September is notetaking month for the whole 6th grade team. Eventually, all the students develop a system that works for them. We don't try to impose one system; we just insist that their notes be accurate, organized, and balanced.

When Eva finishes reading the story, the students break into pairs: one student attempts to retell the story from memory without looking at notes, with the other—notes in hand—coaching with prompts, suggestions, and questions. When the students finish, Eva writes three questions on the board:

- *Vocabulary:* What is the meaning of the word "nincompoop"?
- *Motivation:* Why does the employer lead the governess through this complicated procedure?
- *Quotation:* What does the employer mean when he asks, "How easy is it to be strong in this world?"

Eva then reads the story a second time with the students revising their notes to make sure they have what they need to answer these questions, as well as the evidence to support their answers.

When they're finished, the students break into discussion groups of four or five to explore and refine their answers. As they talk, Eva sits for a few minutes at each table, listening, sometimes taking notes on the discussions in a small notebook. At each table she makes some kind of intervention. For example, at one table she asks the students where they see the evidence for their idea that the employer is trying to bully his governess. At another, she says, "You're saying the employer is just trying to cheat the governess out of her salary, but he gives her everything she's owed at the end of the story. How do you explain that?" After about 15 minutes, Eva pulls the students together to discuss their ideas. She closes the class by asking the students to write an essay on the topic, "What is Chekhov trying to teach us here?"

Reading, notetaking, sharing in groups, and writing an essay is a regular Monday morning exercise in rigor, as well as a time when students learn to enjoy good short stories or other forms of literature.

> Each month I [Eva] use my Rigorous Mondays to focus on a different kind of product. In September students work on notetaking. Every Monday night they refine and revise their notes to fit our criteria of accuracy, organization, and balance. In October we focus on retellings. November is our author study month. This year we're doing Chekhov and our theme is "Authors as Teachers," so our Monday night essays have focused on what Chekhov is trying to help us see and understand in each of the four stories I read to them. Next Monday they'll select their best essay, read it to a peer-editing group, collect feedback, and revise it for Tuesday. It's all very regular and the predictability helps the students. They know what's expected of them each Monday because they produce the same kind of product four times each month. They can see themselves improve,

getting better at producing this kind of writing, or at notetaking.

Rigorous Mondays have many applications. Science teachers use Rigorous Mondays to teach students how to read and retell complex scientific diagrams. Social studies and history teachers devote the period to reading, discussing, and summarizing primary documents. Art teachers can spend Mondays in September teaching students to analyze paintings from the Hudson River School, while math teachers can make any month "Famous Problems in Math Month."

For anyone wishing to try Rigorous Mondays, the program has four basic characteristics:

1. Teachers or schools make a commitment to reading brief, rigorous texts to students once a week (where possible, the texts for each Monday should be thematically linked).

2. The work is read aloud twice—once so students can work on notetaking and retelling, then again so they can explore mildly higher-order questions.

3. After the second reading, students discuss in small groups the meaning of the text in terms of the guiding questions posed by the teacher. While the students talk, the teacher circulates, listens, and coaches.

4. At the conclusion of the session the teacher assigns a product (a set of notes, a retelling, an essay) to be completed by the following day. Students work on the same kind of product each Monday for one month.

The teacher can select any rigorous material in any subject area of study.

Three Scandalous Ideas About Assessment

Ten years ago, when we first began talking to teachers and other researchers about Rigorous

Mondays, some of our colleagues offered objections: "It's too literal." "It's about lower-order thinking skills." "It's too repetitive."

We listened carefully and said, "Thank you. That's just what we wanted." Here's how we have answered their objections.

Literalness. We believe that in assessing students' ability to read rigorous texts, too little attention has been paid to making sure that students can restate and summarize the text. There is a difference between what a text means to us personally and what the author wants it to mean.

Repetition. In education, we frequently undervalue repetition because we're afraid it will be boring. But repetition has real advantages. The more students practice a skill, the better they become in performing the skill. Plus, when completing tasks that involve skills like summarizing, comparing and contrasting, or proving a hypothesis, repetition allow students to see their own progress.

Thus, by downplaying the importance of repetition, we deprive students of the opportunity to see themselves improve by working on one kind of product (e.g., notes, summaries, retellings, diagrams, essays based on one question type). Perhaps students lack motivation because they are not being given enough repetitions to see their own growth. There is a place for variety and choice, of course, but not in the early stages of looking at something rigorously.

Supported Assessment. We have inherited a bias against supported assessment—a legacy from 50 years of standardized tests. By dwelling too heavily on test security, we have failed to see how deeply entwined assessment and instruction must be in the life of classrooms. We want to minimize, though not eliminate, situations where assessment is separated from opportunities for continued learning.

The bulk of classroom assessment should take place in contexts where students have access to a rich variety of supports, including reference materials, discussions with other students, and coaching and instruction from the teacher. Supported assessment validates real learning, reinforces the use of various models of assessment, and increases the likelihood that important assessments will be performed in school, where all students will receive support and instruction in completing their projects. Sending important work home guarantees that some students will receive support (from parents, siblings, and home libraries), while many others will have to struggle with the work alone.

Our belief is that rich, supported assessment leads to genuine learning as well as to improved scores on almost any form of test. Supported assessment is the way to high standards.

Coming into the Open

Many years ago we worked with Michael, a somewhat troubled, learning-disabled high school student. Each day he came to class dragging a knapsack full of books and assignments from other teachers. It was our job to help teach him how to do the work the other teachers had assigned.

The work was not going well. We had taught Michael note taking and the rules of summarizing, coached him through innumerable readings of uncountable chapters in textbooks, but nothing we did seemed to stick. Every day we began again at ground zero. Michael had a particular problem with social studies. He found the history text his teacher used impenetrable.

Then we taught Michael how to make Split-Screen Notes by combining words and pictures. A few days later, after he had read about the Bill of Rights, Michael strode briskly into the room, unpacked his textbook, snagged a piece of paper, and in 20 minutes produced Figure 3.3.

Until that moment, Michael's learning had remained invisible to us. We did not know what he had come to understand about the Bill of Rights, about reading his textbook, or about learning how to learn. We gave Michael a tool for improved understanding and this gave us insight into how his mind worked—he was a profoundly visual learner. Looking back, we should not have been so surprised that we missed this fact. In a certain sense all learning is invisible. Assessment is the work of bringing learning into the open—of understanding not just *what* students learn, but also *how* they learn.

Windows into Rigorous Learning

Assessment is our attempt to construct with our students a window that reveals what they are learning and what they still need to learn. If the window is too narrow—relying only on tests and quizzes—our view is cramped and restricted. Neither we nor our students can see the full panorama of their understanding or their potential.

Constructing windows takes time. Narrow windows—short-answer work—are popular not only because they are easy to mark and seem objective but also because so little time is required to teach students how to take such simple tests. If we begin to ask students to summarize, diagram, construct time lines, use concept maps, or compare and contrast, then we must teach and help students practice the appropriate set of skills The more complex the assessment, the more time it takes to teach students its unique skills and standards. Thus, any significant change in assessment signifies a change in curriculum.

This curriculum-assessment connection has two implications for rigor in the classroom:

FIGURE 3.3
MICHAEL'S GARDEN OF BILL OF RIGHTS

1. It reminds us that rigor is a *quality* of content, not a measure of the quantity of content covered. Rigor enhances a student's ability to learn challenging, complex, and difficult ideas.

2. In designing our assessment system for rigorous learning, we want to select strategies that are not so complex as to distract students from the content and not so restricted that they do not give us and our students a clear view of what is being learned.

Tools for Assessing Rigorous Learning in Our Students

These are not the only ways of assessing rigor but they have proven their effectiveness over the years:

Retellings. Ask students to retell or summarize their learning orally, or in writing.

Diagrams. Ask students to visually represent their understanding of content in concept webs, mind maps, and diagrams of their own design.

Essays. Ask students to write brief pieces that view content through a single critical lens: "Compare the Han and Ming dynasties in terms of the quality of life each offered the people of China. Was there progress from one dynasty to another?" or "What does *Bridge to Terabithia* teach us about the nature of true friendship?" or "What does 21 divided by 5:4 rl mean?"

Notes and Notebooks. Several years ago we interviewed students at a local college who had low SAT scores but high grade point averages.

We found that the one factor that separated most of these students from their peers with lower grades was the quality of their notebooks: the higher-performing students universally took better notes. Not only were their notebooks accurate and well-organized, but they all took notes on both readings and lectures and recopied and revised their notes often; some produced as many as four different sets of notes for the same class.

What's more, they took great pride in their notes. When we asked to see their notes, they would ask, "What class? What year?" Given the complexity of note-taking, note-making, and note-revising practices among such solid students, our cursory attention to teaching students a rich variety of note-taking strategies and using their notes as windows into their understanding is nothing short of scandalous.

Discussions, Conferences, and Interviews. Eva Benevento carries a notebook: it's 3" x 5", spiral-bound, blue. It costs 79 cents. In it, she records her own thoughts and those of her students as she listens in on their discussions, conducts conferences, and interviews them. On one page of her notebook, for instance, Eva keeps a record of how students function in a group. She also jots down notes to herself:

> *Jared*—"Dominator," sometimes overly assertive, trouble with evidence, goes off on tangent when unsure
>
> *Jacob*—better at listening
>
> *Group*—interacts well, building off each other's ideas
>
> *Me*—asked students who's noticing she's crying—What does that mean?

Our fixation with tests, our confusing assessment with tests, does not encourage teachers to take student conversations seriously as a valuable tool. But if assessment is a window, then student comments may be the source of deepest insights into what students are learning and how they learn it.

Rigor in Review

- Rigor is a quality of content, not a measure of the quantity of the content we cover.
- Teaching rigorous content inculcates unique qualities of mind in students and lays the foundation for their deep and meaningful thinking.
- Rigorous learning requires instructional strategies that explicitly target student abilities to infer, organize, imagine, and revise their understanding.
- Assessing student abilities to manage rigorous content compels us to select a controlled variety of assessment strategies that give us a window into student understanding. Students must also practice if they are to see their own improvement in creating specific products.

If you want to see how what we have discussed applies to your own situation, test it against the Rigor Rubric presented in Figure 3.4.

But, important as it is, rigor is not the only standard by which we judge the beauty and thoughtfulness of our curriculum. Thinking, diversity, and authenticity are also necessary. A painter who understands line but not color, a composer who grasps melody but not rhythm, a poet who knows rhyme but not reason cannot create works that are beautiful and satisfying. When we analyze art, music, or poetry by only one criterion, our vision is faulty and flawed. The tragedy of the U.S. school curriculum lies in our tendency to look at the mission of our schools using only one criterion at a time, rather than seeking a balance among a variety of criteria. Rigor is one measure of the quality of content, one criterion, one standard for evaluating our curriculum. A seagull that was all feathers and no wings would not fly. It is time now to turn our attention to thought.

FIGURE 3.4
THE RIGOR RUBRIC

	Level 1	Level 2	Level 3	Level 4
C U R R I C U L U M	My curriculum is textbook-driven and provides few opportunities for students to be challenged by any kind of rigorous content.	My curriculum contains some challenging content, though I feel that there should be more; my curriculum favors one or two types of rigorous content.	My curriculum is challenging, though it may tend to favor two or three types of rigorous content.	My curriculum routinely challenges students with content that is complex, ambiguous, provocative, and personally challenging.
I N S T R U C T I O N	I rarely use instructional strategies in my classroom. Instruction is mostly driven by the textbook.	I make use of instructional strategies at key points in my curriculum.	I make regular use of instructional strategies to help students manage rigorous content.	My instructional program is aimed at helping students develop the skills needed to manage rigorous content through regular use of teaching strategies.
A S S E S S M E N T	My main mode of assessment consists of end-of-unit, paper-and-pencil and memory tests that may not reinforce or develop skills for managing rigor.	My assessment system sometimes separates assessment from instruction; I use a few tools to assess rigorous learning.	My assessment system pays attention to literalness, repetition, and supported assessment; I try to use a range of tools to assess rigorous learning.	My assessment system is committed to promoting literal skills, progress through repetition, and supported assessment. I use a wide range of tools to assess rigorous learning.

Standard 2: Thought

THE PROBLEM WE EXPERIENCED IN DEFINING RIGOR lay in putting to rest the ideas of severity and boredom. Now we face a new problem: the meaning of thought is vague, shifty, and provisional. The proof of this can be seen in a survey of the ideas of a few great thinkers. These range from René Descartes' claim that thought confirms existence ("I think, therefore I am") to John Dewey's belief that thought remakes the world ("Anyone who has begun to think places some portion of the world in jeopardy") to J. William Fulbright's vision of thinking as the key to true freedom ("We must dare to think about 'unthinkable things,' because when things become 'unthinkable,' thinking stops and action becomes mindless"). For some great minds, thinking has even been equated with a curse: Spanish philosopher Jose Ortega y Gassett claimed "Thought is not a gift to man, but a laborious, precarious, and volatile acquisition."

With so many meanings circulating, thought might seem too subjective to define adequately. In our culture, however, there is an accepted test for elusive concepts like thought, or art, or beauty: If most people—particularly people devoted to the concept—believe something is thought-filled, or beautiful, or artistic, it is accepted as such. As professional nurturers of thought, teachers recognize thought when they see it. To apply this test, let's look inside three classrooms where thinking is occurring and see what we can learn from them.

• In the Wayne-Fingerlakes region of New York, 10th graders learn how history is made and recorded by investigating a transitional period in their own lives. By generating information from their own memories, gathering related artifacts, and interviewing friends or relatives who witnessed the transition, students learn how to gather and categorize historical data. Gradually, as they organize and interpret their data, they create a comprehensive and historically accurate portrait of what life was like before, during, and after the critical change. From their findings, the students write a meaningful, interesting, and well-documented piece of historical nonfiction.

• In Ladue, Missouri, 6th graders are studying their own difficulties with percentage problems. From homework, tests, and quizzes the students collect problems on which they have made errors, identify patterns, and then group these problems into categories. In small groups, they use this information to create a short informational booklet entitled "How to Avoid Errors when Solving Percentage Problems."

• In Broome County, New York, 4th grade teachers have organized a two-month study of storytelling in which students compare fables, fairy tales, and tall tales. Individually and in small groups, students identify, discuss, and take notes on the styles, purposes, and defining features of each genre using specific stories to build and test their understanding. At the end of the unit, students create an organizer showing the critical attributes of each genre, explaining why each type of story is written and assessing strengths and weaknesses of each genre as a teaching tool.

A Simple Definition of Thought

In these classrooms, we begin to identify a clearer idea of thought by paying attention to two things: (1) Students in each classroom have a *clearly defined purpose*: developing a personal history, creating an informational booklet, constructing an organizer, but (2) they pursue this purpose *under conditions of uncertainty*. In each classroom, the students must come to an understanding on their own—their paths are neither certain nor prescribed. The students in New York are not shown how to write history; the students have to inquire into the nature of history and think their way through the process of creating it. Likewise, no one showed the students in Ladue the mistakes they were making. They had to find their own errors, identify the sources of confusion, and use their learning to become better students of mathematics. From what we see in these classrooms, then, we can define thought as *the pursuit of purpose under conditions of uncertainty*.

But thought encompasses more than this simple definition. It includes thinking techniques, *disciplines,* for managing the uncertainty. These disciplines allow us to turn preliminary ideas about how to work through uncertainty into deep insights and well-formulated positions. To understand the difference let's look at one of the great works of art of the twentieth century.

Experiencing Thought: Get the Sensation!

Pablo Picasso's *Guernica* is shown in Figure 4.1. Picasso painted this piece as a protest against the Nazi bombing of a small Basque town in Northern Spain called Guernica. Take some time to think about the painting. In the space below it, make notes on whatever comes to your mind as you look at it.

Now ask yourself: What do these notes say about you and your thoughts? Perhaps they say that thought can include simple behaviors like paying attention, wondering, free associating, and forming gut reactions. Could this be true? Could thought be composed of simple, almost spontaneous acts?

The answer is yes. Thought is composed of observation, questioning, imagining, and responding to feelings—all linked in a loose and shifting network. Here, for instance, are the thoughts on *Guernica* of a teacher from upstate New York:

All the weapons are broken.

Black and white only.

Why no color?

Why so many animals?

Disturbing, like *Saving Private Ryan,* all that carnage. Maybe to make people understand the agony of war, you need to shock them.

I wonder what my son would think of this. Would it shock him? Violence doesn't seem to bother him.

I want to like this painting, but it's hard to. I think that's the point—repulsion.

FIGURE 4.1
NOTES ON GUERNICA

Notes:

The elements in these notes are first thoughts, instant cognition. In observing, questioning, imagining, and responding, this teacher was expressing interest in how artists provoke and audiences react.

What if she wanted to produce a more disciplined version of these thoughts for a specific purpose? Imagine that *Guernica* was to be on exhibit in the Metropolitan Museum of Art, and she wanted to write an article for her local newspaper to convince people to travel to New York City to take in the show. Or, what if she simply wished to refine her thoughts as an entry in a journal? How would she go about reaching either goal? Certainly, accomplishing either purpose would require more sophisticated thinking than the first thoughts expressed in her notes.

We are all constantly forming first thoughts. Observing, questioning, imagining, and responding are favorite activities of the human brain. It is the role of culture—especially schools—to transform these elements of first thought into the kinds of disciplined thinking we wish to see from students.

To see how first thoughts become disciplined, let's return to Picasso.

Picasso and the Disciplines of Learning

Picasso did not get up one morning and dash off *Guernica*. That might have satisfied his need to take immediate action in response to the tragedy, but it would not have suited other purposes that were equally important to him: Picasso's need to communicate fully his own grief and anger over the bombing of Guernica;

his need to truly honor the town and its citizens; his belief that cubist experiments of his youth could be transformed to carry greater emotional content.

The bombing of Guernica gave Picasso the stimulus for first thought—a powerful gut reaction against war. But how did he move from first thoughts to *Guernica*? More precisely, how was he able to think his way through the uncertainties of artistic innovation to shape his reaction into one of the greatest masterpieces in all of Western art?

In creating *Guernica,* Picasso practiced five *disciplines:*

• *Inquiry.* Picasso conducted research by investigating his own paintings and the work of other painters who had confronted the question of how to express the emotions of rage and sorrow over war-related horrors—models like Francisco Goya's *Third of May* (see Figure 4.2).

• *Knowledge acquisition.* Picasso used what he already knew about the history and theory of art to organize his learning into relevant categories. In this way, he was able to see how each painting he studied—his own or another artist's—might help him meet his purposes.

• *Problem solving.* Picasso experimented toward a solution that would synthesize his own unique visions with the learning he had gained. He did this by developing and refining a series of rough sketches (see Figure 4.3).

• *Communication.* Picasso understood the need to communicate not only *through* art but also *about* it. In journals, sketchbooks, conversations, and even arguments with fellow artists, he communicated thoughts about how art should be pursued.

• *Reflection.* Picasso continually thought about his own processes as a painter, a problem-solver, and a student of art to assess how well he was progressing toward a solution.

Strangely enough, all these abilities—to conduct investigations, organize new information meaningfully, find and solve problems, communicate, and reflect—make Picasso ordinary, not extraordinary. Ongoing research conducted by the National Research Council into the differences between experts and novices in a variety of fields (reading, writing, mathematics, physics, chess, and history), Bransford, Brown, and Cocking (1999) consistently find the same differences between the thought of experts and nonexperts. Faced with uncertainties, discrepancies, or seeming dead ends, the experts use a repertoire of skills and habits—the disciplines of learning—to strategically find their way to high-quality solutions. These differences are summed up in Figure 4.4.

Why Does Thought Matter?

Thought is how we learn. Thought is much more than the privileged domain of experts. Here is how a 3rd-grader named Katie explained to her teacher how she and her learning partner used visual grids to find factors for 120 using visual grids (see Figure 4.5).

Katie: Micky and I did 3 by 40.

Teacher: All right, and did you double-check it? How did you know it would be the same?

Katie: Because, well, actually at first we thought it was 3 by 41, but then on another day . . . it was 6 by 20 and we thought, well, if we split 6 in half and we get 3, then we would have to double and we got 40, not 42.

What we recognize from Katie's problem-solving process is that students think *as* they learn, not *after* they learn. Thinking is how Katie learned

FIGURE 4.2
GOYA'S THIRD OF MAY

Francisco de Goya y Lucientes. *The Third of May, 1808* (1814). Used with permission.Scala/Art Resource, NY

how to find factors. We have already spent many years trying to recover from our misinterpretation of Bloom's *Taxonomy of Education Objectives* (1956); what we need to understand is that memorizing itself requires imagination, reasoning, reorganizing, *and* practice. Analysis, synthesis, and evaluation are not rewards for lower-level accomplishment but the actual tools by which we acquire learning. When David Perkins tells us in *Smart Schools* (1992) that learning is the result of thinking, he is not going boldly into a new educational future nor stating a new premise, but reminding us of an old one, stated by Confucius: "Learning without thought is labor lost; and thought without learning is perilous."

FIGURE 4.3
SKETCH FOR GUERNICA

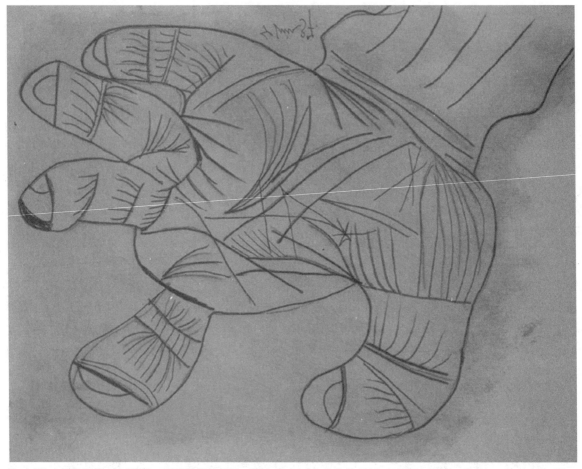

Hand of Warrior by Pablo Picasso, 1937. Copyright 2000 Museo Nacional Centro De Arte Reina Sofia, Madrid, Spain. Reprinted with permission.

Perhaps the question we should ask ourselves is not how do we teach students to think but, how do our current practices in homework, classroom management, instruction, and assessment make it more or less likely that students *will* think.

Thought is what we learn. When experts and nonexperts are given factual recall tests, the two groups tend to perform roughly the same. But when given tasks like constructing arguments, interpreting primary documents, or grouping physics problems, the experts win hands down (Bransford, Brown, & Cocking, 1999). Another way of saying this is that experts perform better than nonexperts not because they know more but because their thinking is more refined, more disciplined.

Treating disciplines as subjects, content areas, is a rather new idea. The older idea—one that needs to be recaptured—is that disciplines

FIGURE 4.4
THE DIFFERENCE BETWEEN NOVICES AND EXPERTS

Discipline	Novice	Expert
Inquiry	Novices are unsure of what questions to ask, what hypotheses to generate, and how to justify their conclusions. →	Experts know how inquiry is conducted in their field: They know what kinds of questions to ask, what types of hypotheses might be fruitful, and how to search for and marshal evidence to test their conclusions.
Knowledge acquisition	Knowledge tends to be a hodgepodge of largely disconnected facts. →	As experts acquire knowledge, they organize it into meaningful patterns around key principles and concepts.
Problem solving	Novices spend little time finding or restating problems. They look for a convenient solution or a routine question and rarely question or reexamine their ideas or hunt for misconceptions, biases, or situations where their knowledge is incomplete. →	Experts spend much more time than novices searching out and defining problems, experimenting with a variety of solutions and perspectives, and looking for holes in their thinking and understanding.
Communication	Novices view communication as a simple telling. →	Experts view communication as a complex process of examining what they know and looking for ways to make it meet both their own needs (e.g., for accuracy and clarity) and the needs of the audience.
Reflection	Novices generally fail to reflect on their own thinking and learning and are often unaware of their misunderstandings. →	Experts hone the power of reflection and self-assessment to expose weaknesses in their learning, to illuminate problems, misunderstandings, confusions, and to determine directions for new growth.

represent ways to think and learn about content and that students become better thinkers by practicing these disciplines.

Citizenship is thinker-ship. Education is not designed to create new members of the history or science department. Public education is designed to create citizens—people who can collaborate to nurture families, build communities, pursue careers, and understand current issues. This does not require that they know the three phases of cellular respiration, or the political machinations of the Meji restoration. Citizenship requires that students know

• Enough about each content area to understand current issues and affairs
• How inquiry is pursued and claims are made in the various content areas
• What kinds of problems a content area addresses and how to search for solutions

FIGURE 4.5
KATIE'S PROBLEM-SOLVING GRIDS

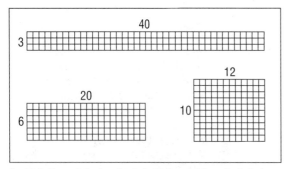

Reprinted with permission from *Developing Mathematical Reasoning in Grades K–12*, copyright 1999 by the National Council of Teachers of Mathematics.

• How people in the various content areas communicate with each other and the general public
• How to reflect and evaluate the implications of discoveries and new ideas in the various content areas

Citizens who have these fundamental understandings will be able to use their knowledge in the decisions they make as parents, professionals, neighbors, and active members of the community. When you step into the voting booth, what are your hopes for the person in the next booth? Do you hope that person knows the facts of the nullification crisis—or knows how to work individually and collaboratively to address our common problems?

Reflecting and Discussing

Figure 4.6 is a chart to support discussion of how thoughtful your school or classroom is. Rate your curriculum on a scale of one to four (one being the least and four the most). What in your school, or classroom supports this rating? What would need to happen to improve it?

Quick Tips for Increasing the Power of Thought

Knowledge Acquisition

• Organize instruction around a few core ideas.
• Model the use of organizational tools like graphic organizers and concept maps.
• Give students a wide variety of learning experiences and media with which to increase their potential for acquiring knowledge.

Inquiry

• Use enduring questions to guide inquiry.
• Teach students how to pose questions and substantiate claims.
• Build research and evidence-gathering opportunities into instruction.

Problem Solving

• Ask students to design easier and harder versions of the problems you give them.
• Set up a high-performance classroom in which students discuss problems they confront and solutions they find.
• Help students see the difference between first thoughts and second thoughts.

Communication

• Show students how to use journals and logs for representing ideas and discoveries.
• Teach note-taking and other means of representing thoughts.
• Allow students to compare ideas in pairs and small groups, as well as in whole-class discussions.

Reflection

• Build units around criteria for growth.
• Write criteria in student-friendly language.
• Ask students to examine work at different stages of growth.

FIGURE 4.6
MEASURING THOUGHT

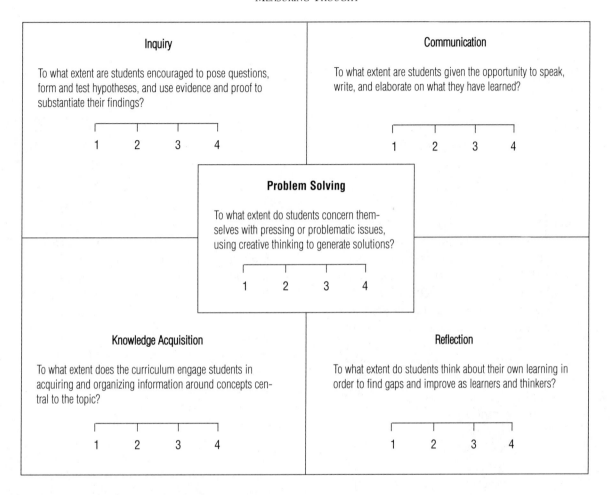

5 Strategies for Thoughtful Learning

IN CHAPTER 4 WE MADE THREE KEY ASSERTIONS about the nature of thought: (1) Thought is the pursuit of purpose under conditions of uncertainty; (2) this pursuit entails transforming preliminary first thoughts into refined second thoughts; (3) first thoughts become second thoughts through the exercise of the disciplines of learning, which everyone—from babies to world-renowned experts—practices, though at difference levels of competence. These disciplines are knowledge acquisition, inquiry, problem solving, communication, and reflection. Therefore, the question central to this chapter is, "How are these disciplines learned, particularly in the classroom?" To find out, we asked friends and colleagues in education a simple question: "Who taught you how to think and how did they do it?" Here's a selection of their answers.

Ito: I don't think I learned how to think until we built our second house. I had been so frustrated with the contractors the first time that I decided to do it myself. I bought some books, developed a plan, hired a crew, and went to work. Well, in three days my plan was in the trash heap. Every day something went wrong: rain, sick workers, not enough supplies, safety codes I had overlooked.

Sometimes eight or ten things would go wrong. I was constantly having to talk these problems through with the crew. Somehow in the midst of all that talk, I learned how to break a problem down and solve it.

Mariko: Father James. I took three courses in college with Father James, and every course was the same and every one was marvelous. In all his courses we read philosophy—Sartre, Kierkegaard, Dostoyevsky. In every course we had to keep a diary. Each week we were supposed to look for a moral or an epistemological event from our own lives. Then we would have to write about the connection between what we'd been reading and those events. That's what we'd talk about in class. That constant process of examining and reexamining my life through my own eyes and the eyes of those great philosophers taught me how to think.

Bob: I learned it at the dinner table, from my mother. She was a single mom, so it was just her and me every night. She was also a fanatical newspaper reader. We got four newspapers delivered to the house every day. So at dinnertime we'd read the papers to each other. About half way through every single article she'd stop me and ask me what I thought about what I was reading and as soon as I said something, anything—BANG, she'd say: "How do you know? Why do you think so?" Bang. Bang. Bang. Over and over. So I'd have to come up with something and then she'd get on me about that. It got to be a game. After a while she'd read to me and I'd go, "How do you know? Why do you think so?" By playing that game I really learned to think.

Jimmy: When I got to 5th grade, I was in real trouble. I couldn't write at all. I just couldn't understand how writing worked, where ideas came from, or how to get them down on paper. Fortunately, I got Mrs. Martin. She did two things that really helped me out. For one thing, she never told me what to do: she showed me what she did when she wrote. Second, any time we wrote something, we would meet in Writers' Clubs. Everyone in the club had to evaluate each other's writing and give each other ideas about how to improve the piece. We were always talking about what makes writing good and how a draft can be turned into a publishable piece. Mrs. Martin used to make sure we were giving each other constructive criticism and paying attention to specific criteria. It took me a long time, but in that class, I learned how to write and how to think.

Harvey: My 4th grade teacher, Mrs. Merrop. I remember two things about 4th grade: we learned to play the flutophone, and that was the first year we had to keep a notebook. Mrs. Merrop was a real bear about that notebook. She taught us all the note-taking strategies she said she had learned in college. We would discuss which strategy worked best under different circumstances. We always began a new unit by putting 10 fresh pages in our notebooks, and we always left the first page blank so we could come back after the unit was over to draw a cover. What I learned from

Mrs. Merrop was a whole array of ways to organize information and ideas so that you could go back and find what you needed. Before that, I never really saw the pattern, the structure of a unit. It was incredible actually, like one of those Monet paintings where, if you stand too close, all you see is hundreds of brushstrokes—but when you take five steps back, you can suddenly see the bridge and the water and the lilies.

The first lesson we can learn from these thinkers' meditations is in the words and phrases that dot all the entries: *every day, continuous, each week, constantly, constant process, a long time, over and over, slowly.*

All these thinkers reinforce the idea that thinking *develops*. Thought isn't an objective to be taught on Wednesday, but not Thursday. It isn't the result of a two-week course on thinking skills. Thought thrives through continuous practice. In the age of standards, it can sometimes be easy to forget that thought is fragile—that it requires cultivation and learning from mistakes on the part of the learner if we expect it to grow. It is cultivated by making thought apparent (Ito's talks with the construction crew, Mariko's diary, Bob's conversations with his mother, Jimmy's discussion with fellow writers, Harvey's notebooks), where it can be refined through examination and interaction with others' thoughts.

Each thinker's story teaches us a specific lesson as well.

• From Ito and his construction problems we learn that *thought develops through conversations about shared problems.*
• Mariko and Father James's journal assignments demonstrate that *thought develops through continuous self-examination.*
• Bob's dinner conversations with his mother show us that *thought develops through reflections on evidence and reasons.*

• Jimmy's growth as a writer teaches us that thought develops in a *communication-rich learning environment where skills are modeled and practiced.*

• Harvey and Mrs. Merrop remind us that *thought develops through strategies that help learners arrange information into meaningful patterns.*

These five lessons translate into specific *thinking practices.* A thinking practice is a sustained way of coordinating student-to-student and student-to-teacher conversations about the processes of thinking. When Bob and his mother discuss the newspaper or Ito works through his construction problems, their thinking evolves because they are engaged in sustained practice, not simply applying fail-safe formulas. Only this sustained regularity of the work in thinking allows thought to flourish (Goldman & Greeno, 1998). The thinking practices described by the five teachers correspond to the five thinking disciplines. Figure 5.1 summarizes the relationships.

FIGURE 5.1
THINKING PRACTICE

Teacher	Thinking Practice	Discipline Supported
Ito	Conversing about shared problems	Problem solving
Mariko	Self-examination	Reflection
Bob	Reflecting on evidence and causes	Inquiry
Jimmy	Working in a communication-rich environment where skills are modeled and practiced	Communication
Harvey	Using learning strategies to organize information into meaningful patterns	Knowledge acquisition

The thinking practices share these characteristics.

• They are sustained. Thinking practices—unlike teaching strategies—are not operations on a single class or lesson, but repeated explorations of the five disciplines of thought.

• They are conversationally rich. They involve robust, but also halting, tentative, and emerging dialogues about texts, tasks, questions, and problems. These conversations take place among students or between students and teachers.

• They emphasize problems of representation and writing. Teachers and students are in constant dialogue about how to collect, organize, represent, and communicate their thoughts and understandings.

• They are both responsive and opportunistic. The teacher neither stands at the end waiting for students to complete their assignments at home nor leads the students step-by-step to an assured end. Rather, the teacher uses the classroom conversations and the students' products and performances to understand their problems and needs. While the long-term goals are clear (ability to think within the five disciplines), the specifics of any class are developed in response to students' thought, knowledge, and skills.

Why do we need to pay attention to thinking practices?

• Because genuine thought is not simply a response to training.

• Because thought, especially first thought, is uncertain and fragile.

• Because, as Vygotsky and Piaget have taught us, thought refines itself through sustained conversation about meaningful problems.

In the remainder of this chapter, we will explore how teachers have used these thinking practices to develop the five disciplines in themselves and their students.

FIGURE 5.2
JOURNEY DIAGRAM

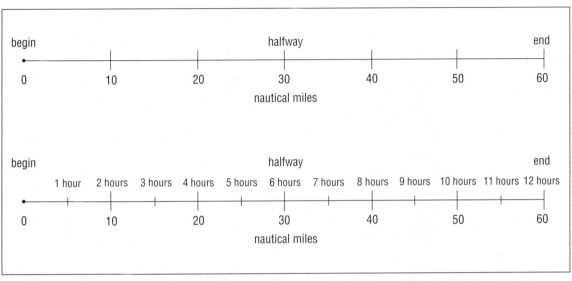

Structured Problem Solving

Late one October, Magdalene Lampert (Hall & Rubin, 1998) showed the 29 students in her 5th grade class how to use a journey diagram to represent problems of time, distance, and rate. Students were asked to think about questions like this one: If a ship travels 60 kilometers at a speed of 5 knots, how long will the journey take? (Bank Street, 1985). The goal was to help students think through the problem using a diagram in which distance was recorded at the bottom and elapsed time at the top (see Figure 5.2).

Over the next two weeks, students used their diagrams of journeys to solve a variety of problems, form and test conjectures, and explain their ideas to one another, their teacher, and the class. Then, one day, the students were attempting to discover how far a car traveling 40 miles per hour could go in 3-1/2 hours[1, 2] when Ellie complained to her teacher that no one in her math group would help her to understand the problem. Lampert turned to Karim and asked him to explain his work (adapted from Hall & Rubin, 1998, pp. 210–211):

Karim: I multiplied.

Lampert: But your job is to explain *why* you multiply.

Karim: (begins to draw, saying to himself) This is how I'll explain it: 40 + 40 + 40 + 20.

---

1. Teaching 5th graders about rate early in the school year is a magnificent example of rigor. Rate problems are often postponed to higher grades.

2. The use of mixed numbers this early in the year is another fine example of rigorous content.

Later, during the whole class discussion:

Lampert: Now one of the things that I saw as I walked around was that something I'd like to see a lot more of. I gave Karim a very special challenge. One member of his group said, "I really don't understand these kinds of problems AT all!" And I went over there and I said, "Karim, can you help this person explain? Can you explain?" (Lampert asks Karim to show the class what he did).

Karim: I drew a diagram [Figure 5.3]. And alls I did was put 40 miles for each hour . . . and I kept on adding by 40s.

Lampert: And how does that explain how you're supposed to multiply 3 times 40?

Karim: Well, like, every hour, you're going . . . 40 miles and so I just added 40 three times, and then it gave me 120, then I had to divide 40 in two, in half, and that gave me 20, so I added 20 cause a half an hour is half of, like, an hour.

Lampert: And did everybody in your group understand what you did there, do you think?

Karim: Well, I think.

Lampert: Well, I only asked one person to really try and understand what you were working on, because I think your group is just beginning to figure out how to work together, okay? Can somebody else in Karim's group explain this drawing? Ellie?

Ellie: Um, it's a good strategy because it says miles per hour and one hour for each one (she points to the vertical marks on the diagram). When you get up to 120 , which is four, which is three 40s, you uh, put a half in there because it says three and a half hours? And, uh, since half of 40 is 20, you add another 20 and its 140.

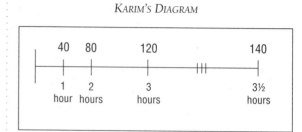

FIGURE 5.3
KARIM'S DIAGRAM

Here we have a transcript of a small miracle: thought in the process of development. We move from Ellie's frustration to Lampert's insistence that explaining is part of the responsibility of thoughtful mathematical work, to Karim's private illustration of his strategy, to his more public demonstration, to Ellie's explanation of how Karim's strategy works and why.

But let's move away from Karim and Ellie's strategy for solving rate problems and examine Lampert's strategy for developing mathematical thinking. It resembles a form of teaching used in most Japanese classrooms (Stigler and Hiebert, 1999), where the teacher works through four steps:

1. Introducing the problem. The teacher selects a type of problem for students to explore (rate problems). The teacher sets up (or creates with the students) a way of diagramming—representing—student thinking on these problems.
2. Posing the problem. The teacher uses one or two problems a day to focus learning.
3. Working. Students work alone and in small groups using words, pictures, and numbers to form conjectures, experimenting to both solve the problems and reason through how and why a strategy works. Meanwhile the teacher circulates, coaching not only concepts

and explanations, but also the social dynamics of the math group.

4. Whole class discussion. The teacher asks students to discuss in public their strategies and their explanations. In this phase, the teacher probes for student conjectures, encouraging them to elaborate on their explanations ("and how does that explain why you're supposed to multiply?") while stimulating comments, summaries, and alternatives from other students.

Stepping Back

Magdalene Lampert understands the need for long-term strategic practice. The nurturing of thinking must occur every day because thought is tentative, fragile, and in need of practice (notice the "ums," "ahs," "likes" and restatements in the dialogue). Thought evolves slowly, therefore it depends on a classroom culture suffused with patience, respect, and interest in others' thoughts. Lampert makes frequent comments describing the culture ("It's your responsibility to explain why you multiply," "I think your group is just beginning to work together"). Seeing Ellie's frustration with her own lack of

comprehension as an opportunity, not an impediment to curriculum coverage, demands patience. This patience may sometimes seem to conflict with standards-based education, but in the end it will deepen students' mastery of the most demanding standards. The teacher is committed to creating an ideal environment for learning, and so Lampert's classroom naturally uses thinking practices to support the disciplines of learning, as shown in Figure 5.4.

Structured problem solving follows the same four-step format regardless of content. Solving problems in the humanities, however, is very different from solving mathematical problems. In language arts, for example, structured problem solving is often used to help students interpret the motivations of characters or to explore how readers construct themes.

Extrapolation

Claudia Geocaris in Hinsdale, Illinois, was frustrated with an explanation task she had given to her high-school students. Here's what she wrote in her journal:

FIGURE 5.4
THINKING PRACTICES IN MAGDALENE LAMPERT'S CLASSROOM

Thinking Practice	Examples	Discipline Supported
Conversing about shared problems	Discussing types of problems, strategies for solving them, and methods of representing them	Problem solving
Working in a communication-rich environment	Regular teacher modeling, as well as words, pictures, illustrations, discussions in small groups, and whole class and independent formats	Communication
Using learning strategies to organize information into meaningful patterns	Teaching students how to use diagrams to make sense of math problems	Knowledge acquisition
Self-examination	Explaining and refining problem-solving methods	Reflection

Worked with kids on what makes a good explanation. Read through several in the science book and analyzed their various parts: statement of the phenomenon to be explained, naming of parts and elements, laying out steps in the process. Fact is, it was dull as dirt. I could barely stay awake, to say nothing of the trouble I had keeping my kids on task. And, of course, when it comes to assessment—they're supposed to write a description of how a cell works—that writing's going to be boring, too. And when kids are bored they don't think well. So it's off to the files and if that doesn't work, Barnes and Noble.

During her search, Claudia came across an unlikely source of inspiration: children's books. What she realized was that scientific descriptions in many children's books are, unlike textbook descriptions, both clear *and* interesting. This gave Claudia an idea.

The next morning she divided students into teams and provided them with folders containing descriptions from a selection of children's books. "Listen," she said to her students, "our job is to explain how cells work in a clear and interesting manner. Remember, we're trying to write a textbook chapter for next year's students. We've done our homework. We know how cells work, right? Well, we're getting there. Then we studied effective explanations in the textbook and identified the key parts of a good explanation." She placed a transparency on the overhead that summarized what they had discovered about good explanations (see Figure 5.5).

Claudia then asked her students to look over the textbook explanations and think about two questions: (1) What are they missing? and (2) Where is there room for improvement? After a few minutes, Claudia asked students to share their ideas.

FIGURE 5.5
GOOD EXPLANATIONS

Good Explanations	How a Cell Works
Describe the phenomenon	How cells achieve the major life processes: respiration, reproduction, etc.
Lay out the elements of the process	Cell walls, mitochondria, nucleus, etc.
Describe the process clearly	Digestion, respiration, etc.

"Well, they're pretty boring."

"Sometimes they try to cram too much information in."

"They can be hard to follow."

"They don't have any—you know—style, flair."

After discussing the responses, Claudia continued

The problem we have is that the examples we looked at are lifeless. They're effective but not interesting, and most of the time they're too complicated to be clear. We need to do better. So we're going to do something new. We're going to study some examples of authors whose business it is to be interesting and clear—children's authors—and see if we can use them as models to help us solve our problem. So here's what I think we might do. Browse these materials in teams and, as you do, try to find answers to these questions [see Figure 5.6]. Whenever you come across an example that answers a question, make note of it. Let's see what lessons we can learn from them.

FIGURE 5.6
ANALYZING GOOD EXPLANATIONS

How Do These Authors . . .	List Examples
Hook their readers' interest in the phenomena they describe?	
Keep their readers from becoming confused about the various elements?	
Maintain their readers' interest and understanding as they lay out the process?	

As the students studied the explanations and identified how authors make—or fail to make—their explanations appealing, clear, and insightful, Claudia circulated around the room to help students clarify their ideas. After the teams analyzed the materials, the class convened to summarize their insights. The result? Well, as Claudia tells it, "When it came time for students to create their textbook chapters on how a cell works, their explanations were alive with images, metaphors, and narrative devices that revealed not only competence, but a deeper understanding of cellular structure and function than I'd ever seen with a whole class before. It was fantastic, fun, educational—anything but dull."

Stepping Back

What Claudia and her students discovered is that the discipline of problem solving is not a set of algorithmic operations that invariably yield correct answers. Problem solving requires creativity, flexibility, conversation, and (remembering the lesson from standard one, rigor) good models from which to extrapolate insights and direction (see Figure 5.7).

∎   ∎   ∎

Joanne Curran's 3rd graders in Ladue, Missouri, also used extrapolation to solve difficult word problems. Whenever students encountered difficult word problems, they attacked them using a the fourfold approach shown in Figure 5.8.

The students were each given the problem on a sheet of paper; they worked it on the back of the page. Whenever they confronted new problems, they referred back to their notes and looked for past models that could help them solve the new problem. For example, for this problem, students referred to earlier problems where they were exploring the concept of grouping.

Multiple Document Learning and the Inquiry Paper

Early in the school year, John Duffy of Hinsdale, Illinois, presented his 10th grade students with this puzzle, which he adapted from Davidson and Lytle (1992):

Mystery of the Chesapeake Bay Colonies

Between 1600 and 1620 the death rate in the Chesapeake Bay area of Virginia exceeded the death rate in Europe during the bubonic

FIGURE 5.7
THINKING PRACTICES IN CLAUDIA'S CLASSROOM

Thinking Practice	Examples	Discipline Supported
Conversing about shared problems	Discussing the problems inherent in the task of explanation	Problem solving
Working in a communication-rich environment	Group and whole-class discussion, teacher circulating to clarify ideas, reading and writing, studying effective models	Communication
Reflecting on evidence and reasons	Justifying claims with textual examples	Inquiry
Using strategies to organize information into meaningful patterns	Using guiding questions (e.g., "How do these authors hook their readers' interest in the phenomena they describe?") and visual organizers to organize findings	Knowledge acquisition

FIGURE 5.8
EXTRAPOLATION IN FOUR STEPS

A 3rd grade class is going on a field trip to the zoo. There are 41 people going on the trip and they can take vans that hold a driver plus 8 people and minivans that hold a driver plus six people. What is the minimum number of vehicles needed to get everyone to the zoo?

The Facts
What do we know?
Vans hold 8 people.
Minivans hold 6 people.
41 people going.
What is missing?
Number of kids in 3rd grade
Number of adults going along
What do we know about the answer?
Number of vans and minivans 3rd grade needs.

The Steps
What steps can we take to solve the problem?
Find out how many people are going on the trip.
See how many will fit in vans because vans hold more people and less vehicles make less pollution for the environment.
Put the extra people in a minivan.
Count the number of vehicles used.

The Questions
What question needs to be answered?
How many vans and minivans does our grade need?
Are there any hidden questions that need to be answered?
How many people are going on the trip?
Are empty seats okay?
Should each vehicle be full?
Can students sit in front seats, or only adults?

The Diagram
How can we represent the problem visually?

= 8

= 41

= 6

plague. What caused these massive numbers of deaths? Were they strictly the result of local conditions like disease or hostile relations between Europeans and Native Americans? How did politics and economics affect the situation? Were all people in the colonies equally at risk?

In teams of four or five, sharing 10 primary documents (e.g., a letter from the third governor, agricultural facts, interesting laws and policies), the students worked with the four guiding questions in the puzzle, which John calls provocations. Different teams approached the inquiry in different ways. Some grouped the documents quickly by topic ("These all have to do with tobacco"); some looked for a sequence of dates; others read each item slowly and surprised themselves with spontaneous hypotheses: "Were they smokers? All this stuff on tobacco. . ." After five or ten minutes, John pulls the class together:

John: Okay, what have we got so far?

Larry: We think it's got to do with Indians and disease.

John: What makes you think so?

Larry: Well, those guys who were found dead in the street. Somebody had to have killed them.

Ang: Yeah, but nobody's planting any food. See here, these corn laws. They get more severe every year. If the punishments are getting worse for *not* planting food, then the people must be refusing to do it.

Siobahn: Why wouldn't they plant the food they need?

John comments,

That's exactly what I'm looking for. It's not just whether or not they're forming hypothe-

ses. Create the right environment and kids will come up with hypotheses like crazy. It's whether or not they're using the evidence. Larry uses evidence but Ang goes further. He's telling us *why* the evidence supports his hypothesis. Technically, that's called a *warrant*. Use of warrants is an important sign that students are learning how to reason.

As students speak, John writes what they say on the overhead—using different color markers to help entries stand apart. After 10 minutes, though neatly written, the material on the screen looks like a jumble of ideas. John steps back. "Okay, how are we going to organize all this?" Here's what he says about this step:

This is important to me. I *don't* organize their ideas. They have to do it. They have to try out different ways of organizing material and see what works and what doesn't. But they work in teams so they have support from each other—someone other than me to catch them when they're wrong or hasty, or to provide a new or just another idea.

After a few minutes the class agreed to use the organizer shown in Figure 5.9.

FIGURE 5.9
RESPONSE ORGANIZER

Ideas	Evidence	Questions
The Indians were responsible for the deaths.	People found murdered in the street.	Doesn't it say the Indians posed little threat by this time?
They were growing too much tobacco?	The laws against planting tobacco suggest people were growing too much?	Why would they plant too much tobacco and forget about food?

The bell rings, but this mystery will continue for two more periods. By the second day the class will have the outlines of at least three different explanations. Then they face another problem: how to synthesize their learning. John comments

> I really want students to be able to write an *inquiry paper* that defines a problem and explains their take on it using evidence from their own research to support their position.

> Over three years, I've collected students' work to use as models of inquiry papers. We don't just look at great ones; we look at papers with flaws, too, and we discuss the flaws. By studying these papers we can come up with a pretty good recipe for how to write an inquiry paper. That's where I introduce the vocabulary: claims, reasons, evidence, warrants. I like to have both their examples and these written examples up front before I hit them with the vocabulary.

> Then I select an idea and we'll write one of these inquiry papers all together as a class. After that it's their job to take one of the ideas the class generated and work it out on their own. This is not a high-performing class. They're good thinkers, but mostly poor writers. I have to spend a lot of time on the writing.

Multiple document learning moves through five steps:

1. Teacher and students together define the problem (why was the death rate so high in Virginia?).
2. The students work in groups to build meaningful interpretations of the documents; to focus their attention on key points, John gives them guiding questions.
3. The class collects ideas from the readings and devises a way to organize the ideas.
4. The class outlines several possible explanations for the mystery.
5. Students study and discuss samples and create a recipe for a high-quality inquiry paper, which they use to write their own.

As this exercise was the class's first foray into this kind of thinking, John acts as a director by setting up the problem, providing guiding questions, and leading the students through the writing process. Over time, students acquire greater control over their thinking; by January they can conduct an independent research project in which they find their own historical problem, track down source readings in both history and literature, and create a refined multidisciplinary inquiry paper.

Stepping Back

John Duffy is teaching his students to think in the fullest sense of the word, giving all five thinking practices a prominent role in his classroom (see Figure 5.10).

FIGURE 5.10

THINKING PRACTICES IN JOHN'S CLASSROOM

Thinking Practice	Examples	Discipline Supported
Reflecting on evidence and reasons	Making hypotheses and warrants using substantiating evidence	Inquiry
Using strategies to organize information into meaningful patterns	Developing an organizer, using guiding questions	Knowledge acquisition
Conversing about shared problems	Discussing the mystery in groups and as a whole class	Problem solving
Working in a communication-rich environment	Constant processing of sharing, questioning, reading, and writing; analyzing Inquiry Papers; model paper written as a class	Communication
Self-examination	Determining what questions students still have; revising ideas in light of new evidence	Reflection

6

Assessing Thought and Curriculum in Student Work

WHEN HIGH-SCHOOL ENGLISH TEACHER ROBIN Cederblad of Downers Grove, Illinois, sits down to plan, she knows she'll start by making a mess. Today she's planning a unit based on Charlotte Perkins Gilman's short story "The Yellow Wallpaper" (1994) and the mess she makes is wilder than usual (see Figure 6.1).

Gilman's story concerns a woman in an apparently loving marriage who becomes obsessed with the wallpaper in the house she and her husband are visiting. Through her obsession, she comes to a new and perhaps dangerous understanding of her relationship to her husband. The story is the first text in a five-week study Robin is conducting this year called Literary Causes: Writing and Social Change. She has plopped herself down to rethink this unit because the last batch of papers her 11th graders wrote, while mostly well-organized, were lacking a deep conception of how to frame

FIGURE 6.1
ROBIN'S NOTEBOOK

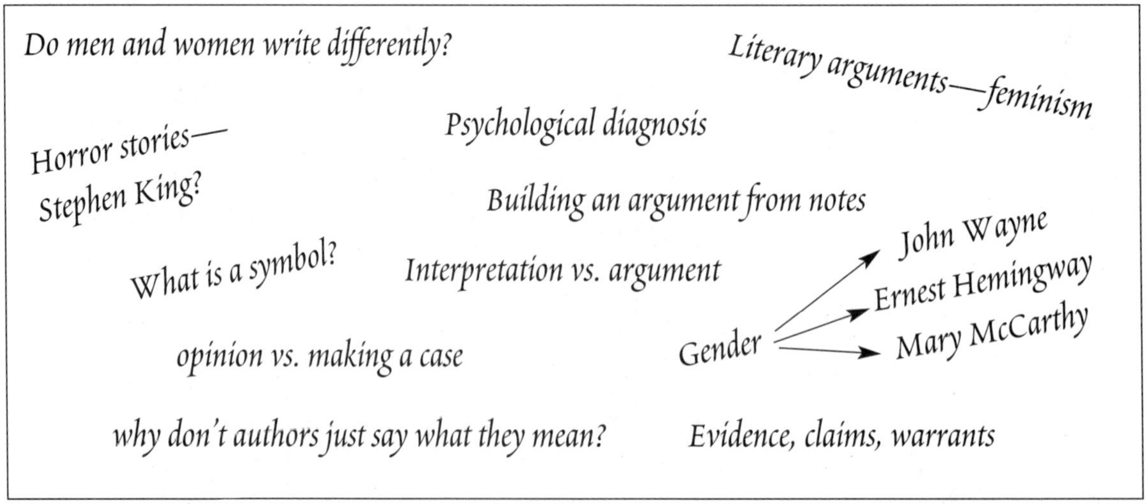

Do men and women write differently?

Literary arguments—feminism

Horror stories—Stephen King?

Psychological diagnosis

Building an argument from notes

What is a symbol?

Interpretation vs. argument

Gender → *John Wayne*
Ernest Hemingway
Mary McCarthy

opinion vs. making a case

why don't authors just say what they mean?

Evidence, claims, warrants

an argument in literature. As she stares at her notebook, she begins to compose her thoughts.

All right. What do I really want here? I want them to be able to construct an argument. I want them to know how to analyze a piece of fiction to see how it works on different levels. "The Yellow Wallpaper" is perfect for this because it functions as a social argument against the medical mistreatment of women and also as a good horror story about sinking into madness. They'll need to read some things about these ideas—Gilman's essay on why she wrote it and something about what makes a good horror story—there's a good Stephen King essay on this. To build their arguments, they're going to need to know about claims and they need a much better grasp of how to use evidence. Okay, this is coming together.

Learning from the Disciplines

As she works, Robin begins to pay attention to the connections between her unit and the five thinking disciplines:

From the discipline of *knowledge acquisition*	She learns to focus her unit on a small number of important ideas.
From the discipline of *communication*	She learns to organize her own and her students' thinking around two central and provocative questions.
From the discipline of *problem solving*	She learns to select a central problem and connect it with the creation of a product (an argument that evaluates Gilman's story as both a story and an argument).
From the discipline of *communication*	She learns to zero in on one part of the communication process (revision).
From the discipline of *reflection*	She learns to establish the criteria for improvement.

Robin plans for her work on a form that acknowledges the disciplines (see Figure 6.2).

These elements—ideas, questions, problems and products, aspects of communication, and criteria for growth—can play an extremely important role in helping establish the aims and structure of a unit, but do not answer the question of how to help students develop their thinking. What kinds of classroom practices are most likely to lead to success in these areas? Let's listen in again as Robin begins to think more deeply about this question:

For a unit like this I'm going to take an approach like the one called structured problem solving. Actually, I'll call it structured inquiry. I need a high-performance classroom to keep kids in a cycle of investigating questions and receiving feedback constantly, so they can see the effects the arguments they're building have on others. Revision, in the sense of adapting and changing writing to meet the needs and concerns of readers, is at the heart of the work here—so structured inquiry is the way to go.

Organizing the Unit

To create the classroom atmosphere Robin wants, she constructs the unit around a series of inquiries that build question by question to the solution students need.

Day One

Pose unit questions and announce the central task.

53

FIGURE 6.2
ROBIN'S PLANNING FORM

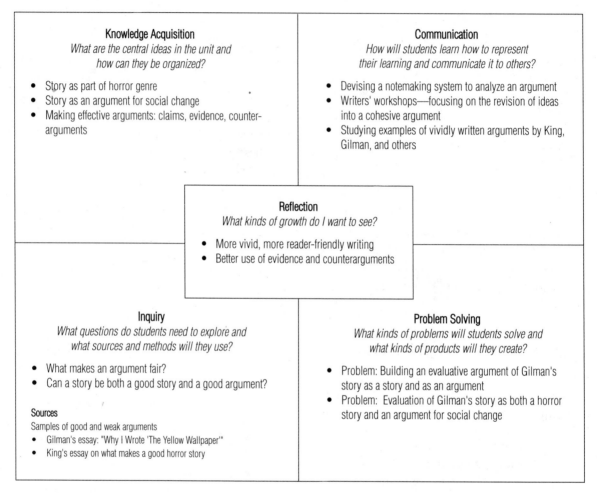

Knowledge Acquisition
*What are the central ideas in the unit and
how can they be organized?*

- Story as part of horror genre
- Story as an argument for social change
- Making effective arguments: claims, evidence, counter-arguments

Communication
*How will students learn how to represent
their learning and communicate it to others?*

- Devising a notemaking system to analyze an argument
- Writers' workshops—focusing on the revision of ideas into a cohesive argument
- Studying examples of vividly written arguments by King, Gilman, and others

Reflection
What kinds of growth do I want to see?

- More vivid, more reader-friendly writing
- Better use of evidence and counterarguments

Inquiry
*What questions do students need to explore and
what sources and methods will they use?*

- What makes an argument fair?
- Can a story be both a good story and a good argument?

Sources
Samples of good and weak arguments
- Gilman's essay: "Why I Wrote 'The Yellow Wallpaper'"
- King's essay on what makes a good horror story

Problem Solving
*What kinds of problems will students solve and
what kinds of products will they create?*

- Problem: Building an evaluative argument of Gilman's story as a story and as an argument
- Problem: Evaluation of Gilman's story as both a horror story and an argument for social change

Inquiry of the day: What makes an argument fair?

Give students examples of strong and weak arguments to analyze and present their findings.

Day Two

Background: Read Gilman's essay, "Why I Wrote 'The Yellow Wallpaper.'"

Inquiry of the day: How can we devise a note-making system to collect evidence for and against her claim?

Day Three

Background: Read Stephen King's essay on what makes a good horror story.

Inquiry of the day: How strong is Gilman's story as a horror story?

Day Four

Inquiry of the day: How do readers establish claims and evidence for evaluating Gilman's story as an argument? As a story?

Days Five and Six

Writers' Workshop: Students work on developing their arguments.

Class examines book and movie reviews to extract techniques other authors use to build arguments that are both fair and interesting.

Overcoming Our Pasts: Thoughtful Mathematics

When 5th-grade teacher Barb Heinzman of Geneva, New York, sits down to plan a new mathematics unit for her students, she makes a conscious effort not to revisit her past:

> I had a lot of good people teaching me math when I was a student—earnest and funny and caring. But the math they taught me wasn't good math. Every class was the same for eight years—"Get out your homework, go over the homework, here's the new set of exercises, here's how to do them. Now get started. I'll be around to help." After cooperative education got to be the rage there was some variety, but not much. I must have sat through more than a thousand lessons like that as a kid. Good people—bad math. They were so concerned with making sure we knew how to do every single procedure we never learned how to *think* mathematically. I did well in math but I never understood what I was doing. I remember hundreds of procedures but not one single mathematical idea.

How Barb Plans

Barb uses the five disciplines of thought to make sure her students know how to think mathematically:

> For me, mathematics is a thing of beauty, something both simple and deep. In math you have to walk a line between the two. You

get too simple and students can *do* the math, they just can't understand it, like me in elementary school. Or maybe it's that they can do the math until they need to understand it. That's when it's too simple. Get too deep on the other hand and everyone gets lost, they don't know whether they're coming or going—they're literally in over their heads. That's why I look for balance. One way I find it is by remembering math really is five things:

Knowledge Acquisition: the ability to understand the relationship between mathematical ideas

Inquiry: the ability to explain and prove mathematical ideas

Problem Solving: the ability to solve problems and learn from your successes and failures

Communication: the ability to reflect on and improve your own mathematical thinking

Reflection: the ability to examine your thinking for signs of growth

When I sit down to plan my unit on multiplication, these abilities, these "disciplines," are the first things I think about. For my multiplication unit, I developed a matrix (see Figure 6.3).

To tell you the truth, most of these ideas are already second nature to me. The real key is working through the sequence of problems we'll be addressing.

During the first week we'll work with problems involving money. I like Magdalene Lampert's idea of using problems like this one:

Make $1 using exactly 19 coins of only two types.

Money is easy and familiar for my students to work with and the idea of combining different types of coins helps them begin to make the

FIGURE 6.3
BARB'S MULTIPLICATION MATRIX

Knowledge Acquisition
Central Ideas

- Move from multiplication as repeated addition to multiplication as a way of working with groups and sets
- Compose and decompose numbers through multiplication and addition
- Flexible ideas about computation with double and triple digit numbers—applying place value

Communication
Exchanging and Representing Ideas

- Math journals with modeled and student-designed problems.
- Work on small group conversations—they need to explain more deeply.

Reflection
Signs of Growth

- Flexibility with multiples and multiplication
- Deeper explanation
- Ability to represent different types of multiplication problems

Inquiry
Questions to Explore

- How can we explain and prove our mathematical ideas about multiplication?
- How can we represent and communicate our ideas about multiplication to others?

Problem Solving
Problems and Products

- Sequence transitional problems from repeated addition to work with sets
- Lots of work modeling how to convert number sentences into word problems so they can build up their own means of representation

transition from repeated addition to working with groups.

Somewhere in that week we'll introduce number sentences, such as 5 x 8. Then, in the next week, I'll first model how to use number sentences to make up word problems and then ask my students to create their own. This gives us a lot of time to explore how to represent our ideas in words and pictures. Then we move onto bigger numbers, perhaps 8 x 94, working hard in small groups to develop appropriate explanations.

How Thought Climbs the Assessment Ladder

In examining standard one, rigor, we spoke of assessment as opening a window into students' thinking. This time let's use the perspective of a ladder. When we use assessment as a window, we are asking: How do my students think? When we use assessment as a ladder, we are asking: How well are my students thinking and what do they need to do to improve? Thought is a developmental process; nurturing its growth means paying close attention to how it climbs the ladder as it becomes increasingly sophisticated.

In formulating rubrics, it has become traditional to categorize student work in four levels—expert, practitioner, apprentice, and novice—so here we ask: What is the difference between how an expert and a novice think? To find out, the National Research Council (Bransford, Brown, & Cocking, 1999) gathered three groups of historians: high school juniors and seniors, college researchers in U.S. history, and professors of Asian studies. Each group was given three tasks: a recall test in U.S. history, an interpretive task based on documents about the U.S. Revolution, and a map task asking the historians to select the map that best represented the battles of Lexington and Concord.

Surprisingly enough, in some cases the high school students outperformed the college professors (especially the professors of Asian studies) on items in the recall test. But the college professors won hands down when it came to interpreting primary documents and solving the map problem. In other words, though the students and professors had similar recall, the professors were far more likely than the students to know how to inquire, interpret, and communicate their findings in a thoughtful manner. Even when the subject matter was outside their realm of expertise, as with the Asian scholars, the professors were much more likely than the students to study the documents closely, question and revise their interpretations, refine their understanding of the documents and maps, and revise the language they used to justify their conclusions. The experts performed differently from the students not because they knew more but because their thinking about history—like Picasso's thinking about art—was more *disciplined*.

Suppose we apply the lessons in this example to our work on the disciplines of learning. Figure 6.4 demonstrates how we can lay out a ladder showing the development of thought.

How Robin Assesses Disciplined Thought

Robin Cederblad uses a variant of the general rubric in Figure 6.4 to determine how well her students are climbing the ladder toward expert thinking. For the task of constructing an argument about "The Yellow Wallpaper," Robin concentrated on the discipline of inquiry because she was most interested in seeing how well students used evidence and addressed counterarguments.

I have to say, we've come a long way already. Using the models really helped students see how to frame and support an argument. But an awful lot of these students don't even mention possible counterarguments, much less try to refute them. For instance, Kelly's essay includes the following paragraph:

Gilman's story shows what happened to women in her society. Their concerns were not taken seriously. Doctors were all males before the turn of the century, and they didn't believe it when women complained of things like depression. Instead of listening, doctors prescribed rest treatments, which drove many a sane woman to madness.

A classmate, Adil, includes the following information to substantiate his argument:

The narrator of "The Yellow Wallpaper" shows that she would be insane with or without a doctor's treatment. Her life is easy. She has little to worry about except how beautiful her summer mansion is or how lush the gardens are. Many people would kill for a life like this. There really is no reason for this woman to be depressed at all. The fact that wallpaper makes her insane only proves she was predisposed to madness in the first place.

FIGURE 6.4
A RUBRIC FOR THOUGHT

	Novice	Apprentice	Practitioner	Expert
Inquiry	Fails to look for questions to guide investigation; generates hypotheses haphazardly; fails to use evidence to substantiate claims.	Can use predrafted questions to direct investigation, but needs help formulating her own; may have trouble telling quality hypotheses apart from guesses; substantiates some claims, but leaves others unsupported; pays little attention to counterarguments.	Looks for and uses questions to guide investigation; uses criteria to generate hypotheses; uses evidence effectively, but may fail to fully address counterarguments.	Can formulate questions and seek answers independently; generates, tests, and refines hypotheses according to well-formulated criteria; uses evidence powerfully and persuasively; and foresees and responds to counterarguments.
Knowledge Acquisition	Fails to look for the connections between old and new information.	Organizes new information into the most obvious categories.	Uses strategies like questioning, grouping, and visually organizing to categorize new information.	Uses strategies like questioning, grouping, and visually organizing to arrange new information according to principles and concepts that are central to the topic and subject area.
Problem Solving	Avoids difficult problems; looks for convenient solutions; rarely questions ideas; rarely looks for misconceptions or searches for gaps in understanding.	Accepts problems on their own terms (e.g., rarely restates them to make them more meaningful); often generates only one or two obvious solutions; questions own understanding only for obvious flaws.	Restates problems; understands there is more than one way to attack a problem; surveys own understanding to determine progress toward solution.	Is constantly looking for and posing relevant questions; experiments with a variety of solutions and perspectives; determines how holes in understanding impede the problem-solving process.
Communication	Views communication as simple telling; fails to communicate learning in a way that is interesting or insightful; pays little attention to needs of audience.	Views communication as a mostly one-way process; communication is usually clear, but rarely insightful or interesting; shows little awareness of audience's needs.	Views communication as interaction; usually balances clarity, interest, and insight; is aware of audience's needs.	Views communication as the exchange and refinement of learning; effectively balances clarity, interest, and insight; constantly checks and refines communication to meet the audience's needs.
Reflection	Fails to reflect on own thinking.	Periodically reflects on own thinking; needs direction in finding and eliminating misunderstandings and sources of confusion.	Regularly reflects on own thinking; is able to eliminate misunderstandings and sources of confusion.	Actively seeks out and eliminates misunderstandings and confusion; charts directions for further growth.

We can see the first signs of this
madness . . .

I can see that they've improved, that they're
learning to take positions and support their
claims, but they've left themselves wide open
to even the most obvious counterarguments.
And it's not just Kelly and Adil. Lots of students have overlooked counterarguments
altogether.

What Robin Does

Robin has an idea. She gives students a copy
of a letter her friend wrote to her sister. She says
to students,

> I was looking over some of the papers and
> one thing I noticed is that we're getting a lot
> better at using evidence. But there's something
> we're not doing. Take a look at this letter a
> friend of mine wrote to her sister about
> whether it's a good idea to sell the family's
> home. And look what she does: she keeps
> saying things like, "Now I know you're going
> to say. . ." and "Of course, it could also be
> said that . . ." She's anticipating and respond-
> ing to counterarguments. Take a few minutes
> to read the letter. I want you to underline
> every instance where she responds to a coun-
> terargument, where she seems to be anticipat-
> ing what other people might say against her
> position.

After a few minutes, Robin surveys the students' ideas:

Mark: She says that her sister's going to say
that the family's house is part of tradition and
can't be sold.

Robin: And how does she respond?

Mark: She basically says that the house is too
much work to maintain. She says, "There

comes a time when you have to put tradition
aside if it's ruining your life."

Robin: What else does she say?

Kemberley: That a lot of people think selling
the family's house is bad luck.

Robin: And her response?

Kemberley: That no one in the family is
superstitious and that old wives' tales are
hardly any reason to stop thinking rationally
about this situation.

Once the class has extracted the main points
from the letter and discussed the importance of
counterarguments, Robin has them return to
their writers' clubs, where they spend the rest of
the period acting as devil's advocates, deliberately building counterarguments to each other's
pieces. Students then use these counterarguments to revise and refine their papers. Here's
how Robin explains the process:

> The purpose of assessment is to help kids get
> better at what they're doing, right? And think-
> ing develops over time, right? So adding these
> two days to the unit—going back after we
> thought we were finished—is exactly the right
> way to make sure assessment is doing its job
> and that student thought is growing.

How Barb Assesses Disciplined Thought

Barb Heinzman's assessment system for her 5th-
grade math students was born out of a frustration with traditional methods.

> Sometimes for younger students, traditional
> rubrics can be a little bit hard to deal with—
> comparing levels and language that's not usu-
> ally reader friendly. Plus rubrics really don't
> tell kids how to get better at what they're

FIGURE 6.5
BARB'S POSTER

You know you are a thoughtful problem solver when you

Inquiry	**P**ose questions to guide your investigations.
Problem Solving	**R**estate problems in your own words.
Knowledge Acquisition	**O**rganize your learning so that it makes sense and is easy to refer to later.
Inquiry	**B**ack up your claims with evidence.
Problem Solving	**L**ook for a variety of ways to represent math ideas and problems.
Communication	**E**xchange ideas with fellow problem solvers as a way to refine your own thinking.
Reflection	**M**ake sure you look back on your thinking process to see where you can grow as a problem solver.

doing. I like to use posters instead. At the beginning of the year, I show my students a poster with each statement keyed to a discipline [see Figure 6.5].

Then I put the poster up, and we talk about it all year long. This poster serves as the class's basic, understandable set of standards for all our work in mathematical problem solving. I attach copies to student work, send them home to parents, and constantly refer to it. It's easy to remember; it's student friendly; and the kids constantly see it and think about it. It becomes a central part of our classroom culture.

Barb also uses this poster to assess student thinking and work. For instance, in listening to her students' explanations and looking in their math journals, Barb realized that the "L" (Look for a variety of ways to represent math ideas and problems) was a problem for many students.

What Barb Does

Barb is working with the entire class on multiplying large numbers, using Magdalene Lampert's (1985) idea of creating number stories and visual representations to make sense of multiplication problems. She writes 5 x 84 on the chalkboard and asks students to make up a story for the number statement.

> **Rachel:** Um . . . Mr. Apple has five orchards and in each orchard there are, um . . . 84 trees?

> **Barb:** Now, how could we represent this? How could we show someone how we're thinking here? Work together in your math logs. See what you can come up with.

After a few minutes, Liam suggests they draw five squares, one for each orchard, and put four trees in each square (see Figure 6.6).

FIGURE 6.6
ORCHARDS

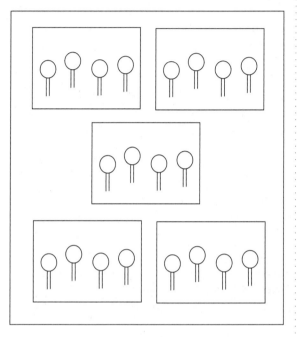

Barb: Does that complete it? What about the other trees?

Liam: Well, um, one day some trucks drove up and brought 80 more trees. Like [Figure 6.7].

FIGURE 6.7
TRUCK WITH TREES

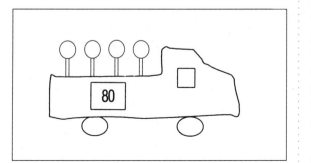

Stephie: Wait, that's not all the trees

Sara: What about the other orchards?

Liam: Draw five more trucks—I mean four more. All have 80.

Barb draws the trucks. And the students begin working out the number of trees in a variety of ways.

■　■　■

So, what do Robin and Barb teach us about planning and assessment?

Three Scandalous Ideas About Assessment

• *Assessment is a way to extend and revise plans.* Plans are not fixed programs of instruction. They need to be refined in action to meet students' needs. Assessment, then, is a way of determining how to respond to the difficulties students face as thinkers. Notice how both Robin and Barb make adjustments in their instructional plans once they assess weaknesses in students' thought.

• *Assessment is both general and specific.* A good general description of thought and the ways in which it appears (like the rubric included in this chapter) can serve as a districtwide basis for assessment. General descriptions allow teachers and administrators to talk the same language when it comes to setting goals for student thought. But assessment is ultimately content-specific and classroom-specific. Notice how both Robin and Barb used the general rubric on thought as a foundation for their own specific assessment tools (Robin's inquiry rubric, Barb's poster).

• *Assessment is not a matter of determining objectives.* Thought is developmental; it grows slowly, over time and through regular practice. For this reason, assessment is not about setting objectives. Backward planning—using the task or tasks you want students to complete as a basis for setting instructional objectives—can make it easy to lose sight of the goal of developing student thinking. Instead of using fixed objectives as an assessment measure, we need to see assessment as a way of bringing student thinking out into the open where it can be interacted with, discussed, guided, and refined. In short, assessment is both a window that reveals how students are thinking and a ladder that helps both the teacher and student determine which way is up.

The Thought Rubric

How thoughtful is curriculum, instruction, and assessment in your classroom? Use Figure 6.8 to help you find out.

FIGURE 6.8
THE THOUGHT RUBRIC

	Level 1	Level 2	Level 3	Level 4
C U R R I C U L U M	My curriculum rarely incorporates any of the five disciplines of thought.	My curriculum stresses one or two disciplines, but pays little attention to the others.	My curriculum usually incorporates at least three or four disciplines of thought.	My curriculum is built upon the five disciplines of thought (knowledge, acquisition, inquiry, problem solving, communication, and reflection) and stresses the connections between them.
I N S T R U C T I O N	Lecturing and textbooks dominate my classroom; students have little time to develop thinking through the five thinking practices (strategic organization of information, reflecting on evidence and reasons, conversing about shared problems, working in a communication-rich environment, self-examination).	I am sometimes able to work thinking practices into my instructional program, but may fail to stress the developmental nature of thinking.	I engage students in thinking practices and talk about their growth as thinkers, but I sometimes favor three or four thinking practices over the others.	My instructional program routinely engages students in the five thinking practices and encourages them to develop directions for growth.
A S S E S S M E N T	Assessment in my classroom amounts to evaluation—paper and pencil tests that have little connection to thinking or to planning.	I try to use assessment to reveal the quality of student thinking but may fail to help students develop that thinking.	I use assessment to bring student thought into the open and look for opportunities to develop it.	Assessment and planning form a fluid whole. I assess student thought by bringing it out into the open and then continually revise my plans to encourage its development.

7

Standard 3: Diversity

DEEP IN WESTERN NEW YORK STATE IS THE SMALL city of Geneva. As you drive in, you pass lush, green lawns leading up to long rows of large Victorian homes that claim beautiful Seneca Lake as their backyard. A left turn into the city brings you to a different world. Here, fast-food chains and discount stores surround a few quiet streets on which thrift shops, coffee shops, and an ancient movie theater compete for the attention of a few shoppers on largely empty streets. Many of the citizens of Geneva are poor or working class people—more than 95 percent of Ontario County's low-income housing is in Geneva—and for years the students in this town were typical of thousands of other students in similarly lovely but struggling towns across the United States.

In 1996 the New York State Department of Education announced that its new standards-based curriculum would be measured on new state tests—tests, for instance, that in high school English required students to write four essays based on complex readings of 1,000 words or more. When the state department announced that the results would be publicized in a new school report card, few of the poorer towns in upstate New York saw this as an opportunity. Most of these districts responded by gathering their scarce resources, working

through some cursory curriculum alignment projects, and asking their teachers to write tests and tasks that paralleled those on the state pilot tests. In short, these districts bet their professional development on the belief that uniformity in curriculum and conformity in testing would at least keep them out of trouble.

In Geneva, they bet on diversity—and the bet paid off. In only three years the improvement in student achievement earned federal recognition. In 1997–98, Geneva was one of only two districts in the country to receive the U.S. Department of Education's Model Professional Development Award; in 2000, based on three years of achievement on state math and reading tests, Secretary of Education Richard W. Riley named Geneva's North Street Elementary School as one of five outstanding Title I schools in New York State.

Here's how Ed Wright, assistant superintendent for curriculum, explained what happened in Geneva:

> When we were first considering making diversity a standard for our district's curriculum, instruction and assessment policy, I remembered how most schools used to have the same mission statement on the wall or in the student guidebook: "Our school is

committed to the full development of each and every student's unique potential." The truth was that most people in those schools thought some students had a lot more potential than others.

In Geneva, we don't think that way. We think different students have different potentials, different resources, not better or worse, not more or less. Understanding these different, diverse resources is the foundation of effective teaching and learning. Of course, we knew that many of our students struggled with school learning. But one of our teachers had attended a seminar with James Collins and she brought back the most amazing quote: "A difference unaddressed becomes a disability." We let that become a slogan: "Let's not let a difference become a disability." Once we had begun to seriously explore diversity as a standard we found ourselves wrestling with some questions:

1. *What do we mean by diversity?* There are so many types of diversity—ethnic, cultural, learning styles, intelligences—that the first thing we needed to do was reach a general agreement about what diversity means and how we could manage the many types of diversity effectively.

2. *Why are we committed to diversity?* This question came from our critics. They wanted to know why, in a time of common high standards, were we so interested in diversity? Wouldn't it be better to simply align ourselves and our curriculum with the new state tests? These two questions served us well. They led us to a definition and a plan for professional development.

3. *What are the dangers in accepting diversity as a standard and how can we overcome them?* This question came from our critics as well, and I am so glad they raised it because it led to a

set of principles of implementation that have guided us ever since.

These are good questions. So let's use them to begin exploring diversity as a standard.

What Do We Mean by Diversity?

We often begin our workshops on diversity by asking participants to take a somewhat peculiar test:

1. What interests you?
2. How well did you do in school?
3. What are some things you learned outside of school in your family or neighborhood?
4. What are you like as a learner? What do you need to be a successful student?
5. What are you good at?

At a recent workshop, a teacher named Alice gave the following answers to the test.

1. Movies, jazz, psychology
2. I was very good in math especially, but I got good grades all around.
3. I grew up in a Lutheran farm community. Everything I saw or heard taught me the value of hard work.
4. I like teachers who are very clear, who lay out what I need to do in a step-by-step manner.
5. Gardening, throwing parties, cooking

Bertram responded quite differently to the questions:

1. Gardening, opera, golf
2. I really didn't do well in most courses other than English. I didn't become a good student until graduate school.
3. I was brought up as part of the only African-American family in a northeast suburb. I learned to question everything.

4. I prefer to figure things out for myself. I don't like to be told what to do. I like to be provoked.

5. Writing, debating, golf, giving advice

These questions (see p. 64) are designed to provide a window into five key ways in which human beings differ from one another.

Question 1 asks about our *interests*—how we differ in what attracts and sustains our attention and concern, what goals we seek, what talents we wish to cultivate.

Question 2 inquires into our *abilities*—where our strengths and weaknesses as students are.

Question 3 is about our *cultural inheritance*—the knowledge and perspectives we acquired by virtue of being men or women, living in a certain neighborhood, attending a house of worship, inheriting different rituals or modes of communication, experiencing different literatures or histories as part of our roots and ethnic heritages.

Question 4 helps us see our *learning style*—not how well we learn (question 2) but how we learn well. There are many learning-style models, all of which describe processes by which different people learn. For example, our own model describes four types of learners: (1) mastery learners, who learn through clear, step-by-step procedures; (2) understanding learners, who learn through inquiry, questioning, and logical analysis; (3) self-expressive learners, who learn by visualizing information, solving problems creatively, and looking for new applications for their learning; and (4) interpersonal learners, who learn best by working with others, exploring feelings, and making personal connections to what they are learning.

Question 5 is designed to expose preferences for various intelligences, the different ways people can be smart as explained in Howard Gardner's theory of multiple intelligences. What

Gardner taught us with his theory was that previous notions of a single, quantifiable intelligence (e.g., an IQ measurement) were simply inadequate to explain the great range of human achievement. Humans can be smart in many ways. Although Gardner's list of intelligences may still be incomplete, he has established eight specific intelligences that relate to language, logic and math, music, space and visual acuity, the manipulation of the body, human interaction, self-understanding, and the world of nature.

Why Do We Value Diversity?

Diversity is important for four reasons.

• *We value diversity because different students need different styles of instruction to acquire the learning we offer.* A common curriculum does not imply a common instructional method. Some students learn more visually; others require discussion; still others favor direct instruction or project work. Attempting to elevate any one instructional strategy above the others guarantees that students whose learning style differs from the common delivery system will suffer. A child who needs an imaginative approach to learning, or one who learns through conversation and dialogue will not acquire the learning he needs and will therefore appear more and more disabled because of the school's refusal to address that learning style.

• *We value diversity because different students need different modes of assessment to demonstrate their learning.* Imagine a student who is full of questions, one who thinks and ponders what she learns. Imagine this student in a class where the primary form of assessment is short answer or multiple choice. Could such a student learn all the material and still be unable to demonstrate it appropriately on a one-size-fits-all form of assessment? Now imagine a child adept at studying, recollecting, and organizing information in a class based entirely on project or problem-based assessment. Both students might learn the material but be hampered in demonstrating their learning because of the restrictions in the assessment system.

• *We value diversity because each child's interests and talents, concerns, and fascinations are the best foundation for increasing that child's ability and motivation to learn.* We have heard stories from many people who nearly flunked out of school because they worked too hard on what they needed to learn. One student built a greenhouse in her bedroom to study the effects of the tobacco mosaic virus on young tobacco plants. Another transformed Georges Simenon's crime novel *Death of a Nobody* into a three-act play. A third put together an acting troupe and traveled across three states on weekends performing a revue he had written based on the works of Samuel Becket and the music of George M. Cohan and Irving Berlin. Everyone who observed the work of these students gave it extremely high marks—but none of this work was assigned in their high school biology, French, or English courses and the school refused to adapt its prescribed curriculum. One of these students was just barely permitted to graduate.

Extraordinary cases, you say? Not so. Consider how many children fail to discover their interests and talents because the school is not interested in them.

• *We value diversity because the operation of democracy requires an in-depth understanding of a variety of perspectives and contributions, as well as the ability to listen and learn from the lives and cultures of a variety of people.* The United States was the first Western nation to establish elementary and secondary public schooling for all its children. In the beginning, the character of this education was determined primarily by a stereotypical vision of a majority population

that was white, Protestant, and Western, but over time we came to see that different groups of people knew things that the others didn't; that it was the combined contributions of many groups that made us strong; that being a citizen of the United States meant understanding a variety of histories, literatures, sciences, and struggles for identity.

In general, these four values call for specific educational responses, summarized in Figure 7.1. Viewed from this perspective, we can see that diversity falls into three categories: *instruction, assessment,* and (combining the third and fourth answers) *content.* In the past, confusion about these purposes and the unique action required by each one has made it difficult for schools to take diversity seriously as a standard. Now we can se the standard much more clearly.

Your Own Diversity

One way to grasp the idea of diversity as a resource is to consider our own resources for learning. Use the questions in Figure 7.2 to begin reflecting on your own diversity.

Suppose you are about to take a course in a subject you find difficult or challenging. Which of these aspects of your own diversity do you most want your teacher to make use of?

What do your answers to the questions in Figure 7.2 suggest about how we might reorganize instruction? Assessment? Curriculum? School schedules and organization?

So, What *Is* Diversity?

The Geneva schools worked out the following definition of diversity:

> Diversity is the goal of helping all students develop to the full their unique and personal

FIGURE 7.1
RESPONDING TO DIVERSITY

Purpose	Action
From the need for instructional diversity	We learn the need to provide students and teachers with a rich variety of learning strategies to maximize student acquisition of required learning.
From the need for assessment diversity	We learn the need to provide students with a variety of assessments to ensure that all students have an equal opportunity to demonstrate what they have learned.
From the diversity of students' interests and talents	We learn the need to listen to and nourish students' interests and talents and to expand our vision of content to encourage all our students.
From our shared need to combine and understand our diversities to build democracy	We learn the need to incorporate a rich and representative mix of contents and cultural contributions to help mold active citizens who respect themselves and others.

The challenge: To use a variety of assessment tools so that all students have an equal opportunity to demonstrate what they have learned.

The challenge: To listen to and nourish students' interests and talents, and to expand our content to include all the varieties of knowledge necessary to encourage all our students.

The challenge: To incorporate into education a rich and representative mix of contents and cultural contributions to help mold active and supportive citizens who respect both themselves and others.

potentials by varying instruction, assessment, and content to both support students in the use of their own resources and challenge them to acquire and understand the resources of others.

This definition has three distinct characteristics:

• First, it acknowledges that certain students learn differently and recognizes the school's responsibility to teach students a variety of learning strategies—both to support students' current styles and to expand their abilities into new areas.

• Second, it recognizes the key role of assessment *in expanding learning opportunities.* A school that varies instruction but clings to a narrow range of assessment strategies endangers those students who may need alternative strategies to demonstrate what they have learned. On the other hand, the definition emphasizes both support *and* challenge, making it clear that the goal is to expand students' resources and to increase their ability to demonstrate learning in a variety of formats.

• Third, by emphasizing the goal of helping students understand the resources, talents, and perspectives of other people, the definition points to the fact that democracy is a learning organization that works by uniting the diversity of its people in the pursuit of common goals.

FIGURE 7.2
SPARKING QUESTIONS

List 10 things you know that you didn't learn in school.	What interests you? List 10 topics, subjects, activities, hobbies that attract your interest or passion.
How does your mind work? List 10 ideas you have about how you think, how you learn, what *your* mind is like.	Who are you? List 10 different answers to this question (e.g., a husband, a fly fisherman, a procrastinator).

With this definition in hand, Geneva was in a position to develop a professional development plan based on diversity. Here's how Ed Wright (assistant superintendent for curriculum, Geneva) describes what they did.

> First, we decided that all teachers (K–12) needed a firm understanding of learning styles and multiple intelligence theory and the teaching and learning strategies most likely to prove effective with different kinds of learners.
>
> Second, we recognized that our assessment strategies needed to change to reflect not only differences in students' styles and intelligences but the changes in the new state tests as well.
>
> Finally, recognizing the role of interest and cultural heritage, we needed to redesign the units we taught our children in the elementary schools and the way we thought through our course offerings in middle and high school. What we wanted here was not only a change in assessments and strategies; we now recognized that content needed to change as well if we were truly going to interest our students and respect the value of culturally diverse heritages we had discovered during our discussions.

Learning from Critics

Were the educators in Geneva finished? Not yet. Not everyone thought this attention to diversity was such a good idea. In fact, there were some very vocal critics. Here's what Ed Wright remembers about the critics.

> Throughout the process of discussion that surrounded our decision to employ diversity as a curriculum standard, our critics played an important role in helping us avoid potential pitfalls. But listening to our critics was not easy. It was all too easy to treat their concerns and occasional dire predictions as signs of resistance—indications of their unwillingness to change. Slowly, however, we began to realize that our critics were important members of our community. They were our experts in anticipating obstacles we would need to overcome—and that difference made them incredibly valuable to the rest of us.

Members of Ed's implementation group foresaw four obstacles to successful implementation of diversity as a standard:

> **Steve:** "I'm worried about the loss of rigor. The more diverse we make our offerings, the greater the possibility that kids will simply choose the one that looks easiest to them. Think about it. How many of us given a choice between writing a cause-and-effect essay or drawing a poster or writing a cinquain would choose the poem or the poster to save ourselves the effort involved in really thinking through the essay?"

Callie: "I'm worried about stretching teachers and instruction too thin. The greater the diversity, the more the teachers' attention is fractured, divided among too many different demands. How will they ever be able to supply instructional support to students who need help when everybody's going off in different directions?"

Sally: "I don't really have a complaint so much as a question: How do we make sure that each student can find himself in the curriculum we teach? If what Callie and Steve say is true, then it doesn't sound like choice is the best option."

Carl: "My special ed teachers are worried about their kids. Though we've always given lip service to diversity, a lot of my teachers have come to realize that mostly what we've done is break tasks down into manageable bites or steps. We're now beginning to think this sounds a lot like teaching students in one particular style. So what does diversity really mean to our population?"

After thorough discussion of these four possible obstacles to the use of diversity as a standard—loss of rigor, diffusion of instruction, variety of needs, and aid for struggling students—Ed's team established four principles of successful implementation:

1. Quality. All curriculum, instruction, and assessment needed to be built around a common set of high standards for both skills and content. This meant that the Geneva teachers had to agree on the precise content and skills that all students needed to master and that diversity would be applied only within this context.

2. Rotation. Instruction and assessment would be rotated throughout units. Models of diversity would be used to alternate the forms of both instruction and curriculum—guaranteeing that over the course of any given unit students would be both supported by working in their own style, intelligence, or interest area, and stretched by being asked to work in areas that came less naturally to them.

3. Focused and Supported Choice. The choices offered among activities or assessments had to be within a narrow enough range to permit teachers to supply instructional support to all students.

4. Validation and Compensation. When a student is struggling to meet a particular content or skill standard, models of diversity would be used to assess the student's predominant style and validate the learner by beginning instruction within that style, using it as a base to help the student compensate for weaknesses in other areas. For example, if a student learns well in a visual mode but struggles with writing, begin instruction with visual means—but only as an anchor to help him improve verbal abilities. In Ed's district they referred to this principle as *style-based scaffolding*. In the next chapter, we will see how these principles work in real classrooms.

8 Strategies for Diverse Learning

IN CHAPTER 7, WE FOUND FOUR KEY PRINCIPLES FOR effectively addressing diversity in the classroom:

1. The principle of *quality* calls for high content and skill standards into which opportunities for diversity can be built.

2. The principle of *rotation* demands that instruction and assessment include a variety of teaching strategies and activities so that students work both in preferred styles, intelligences, and areas of interest and in those they might normally avoid.

3. The principle of *focused and supported choice* sensibly limits the range of student choice, so teachers can support students in their choices.

4. The principle of *validation and compensation* dictates that when a student or class displays learning difficulties, the teacher should use models of diversity to assess potential strengths and weaknesses, then develop instructional plans that validate strengths and use them as a scaffold to support students as they work to overcome difficulties.

A close examination of the principle of quality will show that it is really a call for standards 1 and 2, rigor and thought. Making diversity a standard does not mean sacrificing either rigor or thought. Because we have already covered rigor and thought in depth, we will not handle the principle of quality separately. Instead, we ask you to notice how the teachers in this chapter keep their classrooms rigorous and thoughtful as they employ strategies for diverse learning.

The Principle of Rotation

The idea behind the principle of rotation as it pertains to instruction is that classroom instruction needs to *accommodate* students' styles and intelligences as well as *challenge* students to work in less-preferred styles and intelligences. Let's see how two teachers use different strategies to build both comfort and challenge into instruction.

Around the Wheel

Middle school science teacher Carl Carrozza of Catskill, New York, loves the Dust Bowl.

> It was a terrible piece of history to live through, but for a teacher it's a dream. It's got wonderful lessons in ecology and earth science, great history, and then there's all the literature—*Roll of Thunder, Hear My Cry*, and of course, *The Grapes of Wrath*.

FIGURE 8.1
FOUR LEARNING STYLES

Mastery	Interpersonal
Emphasizes: Memory (knowing) *Looks for:* Specific knowledge and skills *Learns by:* Modeling, exercising, practicing, and receiving immediate feedback *Values:* Correctness and competence *Performs as:* Competent worker	*Emphasizes:* Connecting with people; social skills *Looks for:* Social utility of learning *Learns by:* Experience, empathy, and making personal connections *Values:* Caring and cooperation *Performs as:* Community contributor
Understanding	Self-Expressive
Emphasizes: Discovery (reasoning) *Looks for:* Ideas, patterns, principles, and rules *Learns by:* Inquiry, explaining, proving, and probing *Values:* Critical thinking and problem solving *Performs as:* Complex thinker	*Emphasizes:* Invention (creativity) *Looks for:* Issues, speculations (what if?), ethical and philosophical dilemmas, and creative products *Learns by:* Challenge, choice, creativity, and originality *Values:* Craftsmanship and communication *Performs as:* Creative contributor

Adapted from Silver, Strong, & Hanson (2000). *Learning Preference Inventory: User's Manual.* Trenton, NJ: Silver Strong & Associates, LLC.

When I sit down to design a unit, I know from the get-go that there are lots of different students in my class. I want them all to find a piece of themselves in any unit I design. So I use a combination of learning styles [see Figure 8.1] and multiple intelligences [see Figure 8.2] to make sense of this diversity.

All my students possess all these styles and all these intelligences, but they prefer or have a tendency to use some more than others. That's what makes them different. So when I begin to plan, I use a *Teaching Strategies Index* [see Appendix] to select the strategies I'll need.

For Carl's unit on the Dust Bowl, he selected the strategies outlined in Figure 8.3. According to Carl, "By rotating my strategies, I make sure I 'teach around the wheel' so that all my students' intelligences and style strengths are accommodated, while the styles and intelligences that need development are challenged."

A Jigsaw Model

Sherry Gibbon teaches high school social studies in Penn Yan, New York. State tests not only require students to master essential content, but also demand that students write interpretive essays based on a range of primary documents, including diary excerpts, excerpts from policy documents, maps, paintings, tables, and graphs. These new reading and writing demands are on Sherry's mind as she prepares to teach the consequences of the American Revolution. How will she help students acquire the needed skills? Obviously, a lecture will not do.

Sherry responds by dividing the class into five expert teams that will interpret documents using different intelligences.

• The *Eyes-On Team* will study a portfolio of maps (spatial intelligence).
• The *Personal History Team* will study excerpts from diaries and personal biographies (intrapersonal, linguistic intelligence).

FIGURE 8.2
EIGHT INTELLIGENCES

Verbal-Linguistic (V) involves words and language. It is revealed in an ability to comprehend the spoken and written word and to communicate well through language.
Logical Mathematical (L) involves numbers and logic. It is revealed in an ability to reason, sequence, and identify both conceptual and numerical patterns.
Spatial Intelligence (S) involves pictures and images. It is revealed in an acute ability to perceive and transform the visual-spatial world, a talent that involves sensitivity to detail and orientation.
Musical Intelligence (M) involves music, sound, and rhythm. It is revealed in a sensitive perception of the auditory world.
Bodily-Kinesthetic (B) involves physicality and movement. It is revealed in conceptual control of one's body and the immediate world.
Interpersonal Intelligence (P) involves human relationships. It is revealed in an ability to understand others, to perceive and effectively respond to the moods of others.
Intrapersonal Intelligence (I) involves the inner self. It is revealed in the ability to access and discriminate personal feelings and emotional states.
Naturalist Intelligence (N) involves making sense of the natural world. It is revealed in the ability to recognize, discriminate among, and classify living things and natural objects.

Adapted from Gardner, 1983, *Frames of Mind.* New York: Basic Books

• The *Policy Team* will study excerpts from policy documents (logical-mathematical, linguistic intelligence).

• The *Accounting Team* will study tables, charts, and graphs (logical-mathematical, spatial intelligence).

• The *Arts Team* will study representations of the war and its aftermath in the visual arts and poetry (spatial, linguistic intelligence).

After each expert group studies its documents and formulates hypotheses about the short-term and long-term consequences of the war, the experts join study groups made of one expert from each expert group. Each expert presents the findings and hypotheses of the expert group

to the study group and explains how the expert group arrived at these ideas. As each expert presents the findings, the study group takes notes, listing hypotheses and the evidence that produced them. Following that exercise, students read the relevant section from the textbook, collecting evidence to support or refute each hypothesis. Sherry will then show them how to convert the information they've gathered into an argument-based essay.

Stepping Back

Carl Carrozza and Sherry Gibbon take two different approaches to the principle of rotation. Carl's method of Teaching Around the Wheel has these basic components:

FIGURE 8.3
CARL'S STRATEGIES FOR THE DUST BOWL

Strategy or Activity	Style	Intelligences
Kindling: Students write in their learning logs about "little disasters" they've caused, and share with a partner.	Self-Expressive Interpersonal	Verbal Interpersonal Intrapersonal
Four-Way Reporting and Recording: Using texts on causes, effects, FDR's policies, and solutions, groups of four students record key information using four different notemaking techniques.	Mastery Understanding Self-Expressive Interpersonal	Verbal Logical Spatial Interpersonal Intrapersonal Naturalist
Deep Reading: Students read an excerpt from *The Grapes of Wrath,* select the most important line, explain their choice, share their emotional response, and visualize the line in a sketch.	Mastery Understanding Self-Expressive Interpersonal	Verbal Spatial Intrapersonal Naturalist
Mystery: Students examine documents to describe the situation and formulate hypotheses about the probable causes of the Dust Bowl, the impact it had on people's lives, and how they might solve the problem.	Mastery Understanding Self-Expressive Interpersonal	Verbal Spatial Interpersonal Naturalist
Split-Screen Notes: Students read about the methods used to solve the problem and use sketches to illustrate main ideas and important facts, comparing compare the actual solution with those they generated during *Mystery.*	Understanding Self-Expressive	Verbal Spatial Naturalist
Authentic Assessment: To demonstrate their understanding, students either (1) write a poem or folk song that personalizes the suffering, or (2) write and record a 3- to 5- minute *Fireside Chat* explaining to the country the policies they have chosen to enact.	Understanding Self-Expressive Interpersonal	Verbal Musical Intrapersonal Interpersonal Naturalist

• Strategies are based on models that describe differences in how students learn (learning styles, multiple intelligences).

• Teachers teach the same topic to all students but design activities in the different modalities described by the chosen model of difference.

• All students must produce work in all or at least a wide range of modalities described by the model.

In the Jigsaw Strategy, though the chosen model of difference (in Sherry's, multiple intelligences) is still used to select a range of resources and activities, students experience only one of these activities directly; however, all students are taught from the other modalities indirectly by other experts in their study groups.

The Principle of Focused and Supported Choice

Choice in education is a double-edged sword. On the one hand, choice releases students to pursue their own interests and concerns. On the other hand, the wider and more diverse the choices, the more difficult it is for teachers to provide enough instructional support to ensure that all students succeed. The complexity becomes clearer when we list the choices a student might make:

> •*Choice of content*: "I want you to do a research project on one aspect of the Civil War."
> •*Choice of thinking*: You may
>> Describe a battle strategy, a policy, or a central character.
>> Create a product that reveals the thoughts and feelings of a central character or person.
>> Compare and contrast two generals or battles.
>> Change one aspect of the war and explore how it might affect the outcome.
> •*Choice of media*: You may display your learning in
>> a report
>> an essay
>> a visual representation
>> a series of letters of diary entries
>> a dance or dramatic performance

Given the magnitude of the diversity in even a single project, it's easy to see how stretched instruction might become. How can any one teacher support research into all these different topics, deliver instruction in all these thinking skills, and guide students to a high level of performance in the best use of all these media? Under these conditions the predictable happens: (1) The teacher exiles the work to the home, where some students receive auxiliary parental support while other students receive little or no help and end up creating substandard work; or (2) Many students choose the content, thinking task, and media that seem easiest and wind up learning very little.

What is needed is a more modest, narrower method of encouraging students' interests and choices—a method that permits teachers to continue teaching and coaching both before and after the choice has been made. With this in mind, let's look inside the classroom of another teacher.

Shared Interest Groups

Robin Cederblad of Downers Grove, Illinois, knows why most students don't learn much from the average short story unit.

> First, most textbook short story units jump around too much. Students go from reading a story by O'Henry, to Anne Tyler, to Hemingway, to Poe. These authors and their stories have almost nothing in common beyond their work in the genre. What students learn in the first story they can't apply to the second story, let alone the third, so they plug on from story to story with little or no understanding of what they are learning.

> Second, there's no reason for them to be interested in these stories before they read them. There's no question to investigate, no focus that makes them want to read and learn from these stories.

In response, Robin uses a variation on Literature Circles (Daniels, 1994) called shared interest groups (Silver & Strong, 1995). She begins by pulling together stories to create small anthologies by genre (horror, science fiction, romance, family stories), author (Ernest Hemingway, Katherine Anne Porter, William Faulkner, Kate Chopin), and theme ("growing up is hard to do," "decisions, decisions, decisions," "no day without an epiphany"). She begins with the family stories genre, asking students to tell family stories of their own in small groups. Using a few of these stories, the class identifies criteria for a good family story.

Robin then gives students short excerpts from four different family stories in her anthology along with a "2/3 synopsis"—a two-paragraph summary of the first two-thirds of the story. Students use the excerpts and the synopses to rank the stories in order of interest to them, writing down their reasons in their journals.

Students move around the room to discuss their interests. Gradually, they form readers' groups based on shared interests. Within these groups they read the family story they selected, and collaborate to take notes to help them answer a focus question (e.g., what does the author want us to learn about families?), and present their findings to the class.

Students read all four family stories and write an essay arguing which is the best in the genre, explaining the qualities they admire in the story they chose as the best and the weaknesses in the other stories.

Robin then expands the structure to a broader genre study. Students read descriptions of the horror, romance, and science fiction genres, along with brief descriptions of the four stories they will read if they select that genre. Once again, students rank choices and form groups based on common interests. For the next week, they work in their groups to discuss and collect notes on the techniques authors use to make their work representative of the genre. Each group presents its findings to the class.

Robin says, "I present three two-week units like this during the year: one on genre, one on authors, and one on theme. By the end of the year my students not only know the short story, they know what they like and what they want to read more of as well."

Robin's shared interest groups work because they

- Respond to student interests, but within a manageable range.
- Permit students to make one choice—the choice of content—but keep choices of media and the style of thinking constant for the whole class.
- Begin with shared, not individual, interests.
- Focus on student work—in reading, note-taking, discussion, writing, and preparing their presentations—that is performed in class.

These four components make it possible for teachers to model and coach all aspects of student work in small groups and by conferencing, rather than dispersing their efforts over a too-broad range of choices.

What should be obvious is how these same components can be applied to a wide variety of situations.

- A social studies teacher could choose one content (causes of the Civil War) and one genre or media (facsimile diaries of citizens from two sides of the conflict), but form shared interest groups around different types of thinking (diaries that report incidents, argue for a side, speculate on possible changes and effects, or explore the feelings of people caught up in the war).
- A math teacher might keep constant the content (probability) and the activity (problem solving) but form shared interest groups around different media for demonstrating solutions.
- An art teacher might hold constant the medium (watercolor) and the thinking

(investigating perspective), but form shared interest groups around content, with groups exploring still lifes, landscapes, people, and abstract forms.

• A science teacher could hold constant the genre (lab report), keep everybody working on the same thinking activity (dissection), but build shared interest groups around different content (frogs vs. rabbits, circulatory systems vs. reproductive systems).

• An elementary teacher could establish a common theme (friendship) and a common genre (an advice book on how to be a good friend) but form shared interest groups around different readings (Arnold Lobel's *Frog and Toad* books or James Marshall's *George and Martha* books or Russell Hoban's *Frances* series).

The Principle of Validation and Compensation

Helping a Struggling Writer

In *Strategies for Struggling Writers* (1997), James L. Collins tells of Brandon, a learning-disabled 9th-grader who couldn't grasp how topic sentences and support sentences work together to make coherent paragraphs. When asked, "Do you think professional athletes get paid too much or too little for their jobs?" Brandon gave the following response.

> Salaries, do you think someone who works 3 hours a week for 16 week deserve $2.6 million dollars. The person works 48 hours total and earns each hour $54,166,67. No one should earn that much money. Another person who makes too much for not enough work. Kevin Gogan just signed a contract for $3.6 million dollars for 3 years. No one dervise to earn that much money especially when people who work twice as hard don't make even close to that much money. I think

something is wrong her. (From *Strategies for Struggling Writers* pp. 65–73 by J. L. Collins, 1998, New York: The Guilford Press. Copyright 1998 by James L. Collins. Reprinted with permission.)

But only a few months later, Brandon wrote, revised, and edited this news summary with only minimal help:

> This is a short article about business opportunities for Americans in South Africa. It reports that the economic climate in South Africa is quickly improving after years of sanctions. Business opportunities are especially strong for African-American-owned firms because South Africa offers an untapped market of 45 million consumers. Two major black-owned companies, a manufacturer of hair-care products and an investment-management firm have already started doing business there. Many hundreds of small companies and entrepreneurs and consultants are also doing business there.
>
> In my opinion business opportunities for Americans in South Africa are a very positive sign. Both Americans and South Africans benefit from the involvement of American business in South Africa. American business people, especially African Americans, have a new market for their goods and services, South Africans have new products and services to improve their lives. This favorable business climate will help to stabilize the new political structure in South Africa. (From *Strategies for Struggling Writers* pp. 65–73 by J. L. Collins, 1998, New York: The Guilford Press. Copyright 1998 by James L. Collins. Reprinted with permission.)

Collins had recognized that Brandon was a Mastery learner who preferred to work in a step-by-step manner with lots of teacher modeling. But the change came when it occurred to

Collins that Brandon was a visual, not a linguistic, learner. Collins had been telling Brandon how to write—even showing him, in writing, what to do. Now Collins asked himself if he could somehow make Brandon's lessons more visual. He began to pursue another strategy in which he and Brandon coauthored responses and then analyzed these responses visually by drawing arrows connecting main ideas to supporting details and sentences. They then connected repeated or similar words and ideas to each other so that all the information led back to the boxed main idea, as shown in Figure 8.4.

Collins suggested that Brandon start seeing the act of connecting sentences as "drawing a map." This idea really helped Brandon and he replied, "Yeah, X marks the spot and everything leads to X."

What made the difference? Two words: validation and compensation. Collins recognized Brandon's weakness as a linguistic learner and taught him how to use visual acuity to compensate for difficulty in the verbal domain. As a result, Brandon's linguistic abilities showed a remarkable improvement.

Validation, Compensation, and Science

Talented and vivacious, Wende Brock had been a successful science teacher for 10 years. Then in 1988 she met a class that drove her to distraction and made her question her own competence. Her 5th period class caused her to doubt not only her ability to teach but even her ability to manage the classroom. Though happy and friendly, these students would not—could not—stop talking, no matter how many names went up on the board and how many marks followed those names.

Wende gave the class the Learning Preference Inventory (Hanson & Silver, 1991) and made a special effort to chat with them before and after class. The LPI gave her two critical pieces of information: (1) three-quarters of her

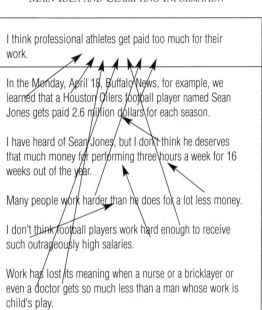

FIGURE 8.4
MAIN IDEA AND CLARIFYING INFORMATION

class were interpersonal learners, and (2) five-sixths of the class were extroverts. With these two pieces of information in mind, she understood both their strengths and their weaknesses (see Figure 8.5).

With these ideas in mind, Wende developed the plan outlined in Figure 8.6.

Is Math a Worst-Case Scenario for Diversity?

From a traditional perspective, there might seem to be little room for principles of diversity in mathematics, so how well do these applications translate to the teaching of mathematics? Let's consider Barb Heinzman's 5th-grade math class.

FIGURE 8.5
WENDE BROCK'S SCIENCE CLASS

Potential Strengths	Potential Weaknesses
• Work together well in groups. • Are good team members. • Know how to encourage and delight each other. • Judge the value of knowledge in terms of how it might be used in their communities.	• Have difficulty extracting critical information from texts and lectures. • Need to talk about ideas in order to understand them. • Learn best from people with whom they have an ongoing relationship. • See little value in abstract terms and academic concepts.

The SPEAR Model

Barb's classroom has three noticeably separate sections. Several desks up front have been pushed together to make a larger table where eight students are working with Barb. Near the middle of the room another nine students work in rows of three. By the windows there are large tables full of balances, measuring cups, graph paper, tapes, scissors, and twelve large cranberry juice jars that glint in the sun where the third group works. Barb explains the physical arrangements of the classroom:

This is my estimation unit. The kids are divided into three heterogeneous teams. At any time one group will be working at the back of the room in the math lab. Today, they're estimating the number of items in gallon jars of beans, rice, alphabetini, and Kosher salt. Working out a sound estimate for each different kind of jar is progressively harder, and the score they earn is a ratio of the accuracy of their estimation to the time it takes them to do it. Then another group works in the rows here practicing

FIGURE 8.6
WENDE'S PLAN

Validate and Compensate	
Increase the role of collaborative learning ⟶	**But** focus that learning on how to take notes on reading and lectures as well as how to pass quizzes and complete homework.
Place students in teams for six weeks at a stretch ⟶	**But** post grades as a bar graph. How many students scored in the 90s, the 80s, etc. Then discuss how to improve scores without simplifying tests.
Create project work that has direct application in the community ⟶	**But** include methods that measure the quality of work in terms of correct use of concepts and other important study skills.

computation skills on their own; 30 percent of their work is a review of other skills from previous units. The final group meets up front with me in seminar.

Seminar is where we explore and discuss new concepts. I usually begin by posing a problem and asking students to attempt to solve it using drawings, manipulatives, and journal writing. I find that by sitting with a small group I can observe better what they're up to and how their thinking is going. Also, a small group allows for a lot better discussion than when the whole class is involved. I used to group the students homogeneously—a high, medium, and low group—but I found that heterogeneous groups work a lot better for everyone.

When seven to ten days' work is done, we'll move to an application phase for about a week. In the application phase we'll apply what we've learned about estimation to a real-life project. This year I think we'll try to estimate how many breaths the student body takes each day. In the past we've tried to estimate the number of different species of plants there are on the school lawn and the number of birds that pass over the school during the migrations in the fall."

This is the SPEAR model spelled out in Figure 8.7.

Why does Barb Heinzman teach math this way? Barb's teaching was influenced by Ed Thomas. From Thomas, Barb learned that different students have different styles of mathe-

FIGURE 8.7
THE SPEAR MODEL

Seminars to Discuss New Ideas
+
Practice for Computational Accuracy
+
Explorations to Build Problem Solving Skills
+
Applications in the Real World
=
Real Math Understandings

matical learning. In the Thomas model, students approach mathematics in four different ways (see Figure 8.8). Barb's comments explain her interest in the Thomas model:

> What I saw right away was that not only did different students approach mathematics using different learning styles, but real mathematical power required using all four styles. Think about it: If you can't compute accurately, explain your ideas, discover solutions, and apply math in the real world—you don't know math. Miss even one of these and you miss the boat. The problem with most math programs is they emphasize just one of these and leave out the rest. By building every unit so it includes all four styles of learning, I support all my students and I stretch them into areas where they wouldn't naturally go.

FIGURE 8.8
THE MATH STYLES MODEL

ST-Mastery	SF-Interpersonal
The Mastery math student wants a no-nonsense approach to math. This student wants to be told exactly what to do and how to do it.	The Interpersonal student wants a social and hands-on approach to learning math. This student wants to work with a partner or team to solve real-world problems.
The Mastery student learns math best through	The Interpersonal student learns math best through
• Step-by-step processes • Well-defined practice and drill • Direct instruction • Straightforward and impartial assessment	• Manipulatives and games • Group activities • Real-world math activities • Assessment that emphasizes the social utility of math
NT-Understanding	**NF-Self-Expressive**
The Understanding math student wants to know why math works. This student wants to see which definitions, properties, or theorems justify the conclusions and results.	The Self-Expressive math student wants to discover what if . . . This student wants to apply math concepts in new, exciting, and creative ways.
The Understanding student learns math best through	The Self-Expressive student learns math best through
• Definitions, postulates, and theorems • Verifications and proofs • Problems with rigor • Assessment that challenges students to demonstrate full understanding	• Creative projects • Personal discoveries • Math problems of interest • Assessment that rewards creativity and innovation

Adapted from Thomas, 1999. *Styles and Strategies for Teaching High School Mathematics.* Trenton, NJ: The Thoughtful Education Press, LLC. Reprinted with permission from the publisher.

9

Assessing Diversity in Curriculum and Student Work

THROUGHOUT OUR DISCUSSION OF DIVERSITY WE have emphasized ways in which learning style, multiple intelligences, culture, and interest can enhance students' motivation and learning when used with the principles of quality, rotation, focused and supported choice, and validation and compensation. Now we explore how these principles relate to assessment, and how diversity is applied to the tricky problems of curriculum and school structure (how we organize courses, schedule classes, and group students).

These problems pertaining to diversity's relationship to assessment, curriculum, and structure are tricky because the more we diversify student learning, the greater the possibility of creating different standards for different students and the greater the danger that these standards become high standards for some students and low standards for others. Take assessment, for example. Imagine a 5th grade teacher whose class has just finished reading Katherine Paterson's *Bridge to Terabithia*, a rigorous and challenging novel for 5th graders—and for most adults. If the students then have a choice between the following assessment tasks, it's easy to see the problem:

• Write an essay in which you discuss the meaning of "devotion" in Jessie's and Leslie's relationship.

• Create a poster that illustrates the nature of Jessie's and Leslie's friendship.

The first task will assess ability to write in a meaningful way about a complex concept (devotion); the second asks students to illustrate a far more familiar idea (friendship). Students who are uncertain about their writing abilities, or are puzzled and unsure of how the concept of devotion changes throughout the novel will obviously choose the poster task or write about friendship, thereby working toward a lower— not merely a different—standard. What's more, by offering the two tasks as equivalent, the teacher must treat student work on tasks as equivalent in quality—even if he knows this is not the case.

The same phenomenon—different standards for different children—operating at a school or district level causes real damage to student learning. In her landmark study, *Keeping Track: How Schools Structure Inequality* (1985), Jeannie Oakes asked secondary students from high-track and low-track courses the most important thing they had learned in school. The students from high-track courses in a variety of content areas gave these responses:

• I think the most important thing I've done in this class is exercise my brain. To work out problems logically so I can learn to work out problems later in life logically.

• I have proved to myself that I have the discipline to take a difficult class just for the knowledge, even though it has nothing to do with my career plans.

• To understand concepts and ideas and experiment with them. Also, to work independently.

• How to express myself through writing and being able to compose the different thoughts in a logical manner; this is also a class where I may express my creativity.

Here's a sample of responses from students in low-track classes, also in a variety of content areas:

• The most important thing I have learned in this class is to always have your homework in and have materials ready whenever she is ready.

• Manners.

• I think the most important is coming into class and getting our folders and going to work.

• Behave in class.

These answers might have been attributed to differences in students' abilities, but Oakes then asked teachers about the goals of their courses for low-track and high-track students. This is what some of the teachers of high-track students said:

• Problem-solving situations—made to think for themselves. Realizing importance of their education and use of time. Easy way is not always the best way.

• Ability to reason logically in all subject areas.

• The art of research.

• To think critically—to analyze, ask questions.

In contrast, teachers of low-track classes responded:

• I want them to respect my position—if they'll get this, I'll be happy.

• Business-oriented skills—how to fill out a job application.

• To learn how to follow one set of directions at a time, take a directive order and act upon it.

• Content—minimal. Realistic about goals. Develop ones they can achieve. [*From Keeping Track: How Schools Structure Inequality* (pp. 67–90), by J. Oakes, 1985, New Haven, CT: Yale University Press. Copyright 1985 by Yale University Press. Reprinted and excerpted with permission.]

What we have here again is a differentiated curriculum—a differentiation that occurs as high standards for some students, low standards for the rest. What was a simple mistake in assessment offerings for *Bridge to Terabithia* has been transformed into a principle for organizing an entire school structure—a principle that reduces how much and how well a significant number of students learn. The question is: How do we honor diversity and maintain high standards for all students?

Task Rotation

When Abigail Silver designed her 5th grade unit on *Bridge to Terabithia*, she asked her students to perform assessment tasks in each of the four learning styles (see Figure 9.1).

The first task was performed early in the unit, the second somewhat later, and the last two near the unit's end. All the work was done in class, both in collaborative groups and independently; Abigail was available to provide support for students working outside their style of competence, but all students were required to perform all four tasks. In this way, Abigail both validated and challenged every

FIGURE 9.1
FOUR ASSESSMENT TASKS FOR 5TH GRADERS

Mastery (Task 1)	Interpersonal (Task 4)
Create a character matrix to collect information about the main characters (Jesse, Leslie, Mrs. Meyers, Wanda Kay, and Janice). Collect information about the (a) physical characteristics and (b) actions of each character. Then, based on your observations, (c) speculate about what is going on inside each character—what their feelings are and the motivations for their behavior.	Write a friendly letter of persuasion to convince your friend to read *Bridge to Terabithia*. Think about what you know of your friend's personality. Try to raise curiosity about the book so that your friend will be convinced he needs to read this novel.
Understanding (Task 3)	**Self-Expressive (Task 2)**
Psychologists list three general stages to the grief process that every person goes through when she loses a loved one—shock, suffering, recovery. Pretend that Katherine Paterson has not yet published *Bridge to Terabithia*. She has hired you to prove that Jesse's reactions to Leslie's death are emotionally natural and typical. Using the reading on the three stages of grief, read the chapter again, and collect evidence. Present your findings and suggestions in a report.	Select one of the following objects to compare to Jesse: microscope rope mirror puzzle Explain why your chosen object is a good metaphor for Jesse and his personality.

student's learning style and applied the principle of validation and compensation.

Carl Carrozza of Catskill, New York, uses four aspects of multiple intelligence theory to create an assessment for his 7th grade science students:

Task 1—Spatial Intelligence. *APW Wants You!* The Army of Physical Workers wants you to design a recruitment poster. Your poster must include a slogan, four illustrations of physical work, a written section describing the kind of people APW wants to hire, and a good, scientifically sound description of the kinds of physical work involved.

Task 2—Bodily/Kinesthetic Intelligence. *That's Not Work!* Two students are arguing that isometric exercise is more/less beneficial than weight training. With a classmate complete two exercises, one using weights, the other using isometrics. Discuss which workout was more strenuous, which was more beneficial, and which would be considered work according to scientific principles. (You may argue that both or neither are work, provided you use evidence.) Then, take a side in the argument, or argue against both.

Task 3—Logical/Mathematical Intelligence. *Chimney construction analysis:* You have been asked to replace four chimney tops on an old mansion. The roof is eight meters above the ground and each chimney top will be one meter high. Each will require 100 bricks and 200 kgs.

of mortar. Each brick is 10 centimeters square and weighs one kilogram.

- Identify all aspects that require physical work.
- Calculate the total mass of all materials.
- Calculate how much force will be needed to lift the materials.
- Suggest a method for the workers to lift the materials.
- Calculate the total distance materials will be moved.
- Calculate how much work (in joules) is needed to position the materials on the roof.

Task 4—Linguistic Intelligence. *The New Fables of Aesop*. Silver Publishing Co. is interested in fables written by new authors. Read two fables and analyze their characteristics. Next, look over some of the key principles of work we have studied. Write a fable based on one of these principles. Your fable should teach the principle in an interesting way and demonstrate your scientific understanding of physical work.

Sherry Gibbon of Penn Yan, New York, uses a model of cultural difference to create the following assessment task for her U.S. history students:

> Revise the chapter on the Civil War in our textbook to show the effects and contributions of the Civil War on one of the following groups of people: (a) Native Americans in the South and West; (b) African Americans who remained on the plantations; (c) women who remained at home; or (d) the ordinary soldier in the North and South.

One of the haunting questions in school reform is the extent to which diversity is possible or desirable in mathematics. We have already seen how Barb Heinzman's classroom operates. Several recent award-winning math series have also seen the need for a diversity of approaches to math, including *Connected Math* (Lappan et al., 1998), *MathScape* (From Zero to One and Beyond: Teacher's Guide, 1998), and *Math In Context* (Packages and Polygons, 1998). For instance, while investigating fractions, decimals, and percents, students using *Bits and Pieces II* (Lappan et al., 1998) engage in the activities described in Figure 9.2.

What the examples all have in common are the principles we have been examining throughout our discussion of diversity:

- They all conform to a set of common high standards (the principle of quality).
- They seek to assess students' understanding by asking them to work in a variety of modalities—both areas of strength and areas of weakness (the principle of rotation).
- In most cases, they allow students to select the tasks they wish to complete, but choices are limited to allow the teacher to effectively support each student (the principle of focused and supported choice).
- Whenever students are challenged to work outside preferred learning styles, multiple intelligences, or interests, the teachers establish connections to the students' preferred styles, intelligences, and interests (the principle of validation and compensation).

But where does ability fit into this picture? Although it is both irresponsible and unwise to deny the differences in students' abilities, it is unethical to regard ability as a fixed limit on what a student can do, because

- Ability ignores the effects of student effort, motivation, and interest.
- Ability ignores the effects of learning style, teaching style, and multiple intelligences, thereby sidelining how student performance might improve in response to changes in instruction and assessment.
- Ability transforms undeniable differences in performance as reader, writer, and problem

FIGURE 9.2
MATH TASKS AND ACTIVITIES

In-Class Test

Kristine, a high-school student, works part time at the dry cleaners. Her take-home check is $80 every two weeks. She has set up this budget for herself:

- 1/3 of her paycheck goes into her college savings account
- 1/4 of her paycheck is for clothing
- 1/6 of her paycheck is for snacks
- 1/4 of her paycheck is for entertainment and recreational activities with friends

1. What dollar amount of her paycheck goes to each of the following areas?

savings? _____clothing? _____

snacks?_____entertainment? _____

2. Make a circle graph showing Kristine's budget.

Self-Assessment

1. Of the vocabulary words I defined or described in my journal, the word _____ best demonstrates my ability to give a clear definition or description. Of the vocabulary words I defined or described in my journal, the word _____ best demonstrates my ability to use an example to help explain or describe an idea.

2. These are the mathematical ideas I am still struggling with:

3. This is why I think these ideas are difficult for me:

4. Here are page numbers of journal entries that give evidence of what I am struggling with, along with descriptions of what each entry shows:

Explaining Why

1. Choose one of the items you ordered. List the item with a brief description and give its price.

2. What would this item cost if it were on sale for 25% off? Show how you found your answer.

3. What would the item cost if it were on sale for 1/3 off? Show how you found your answer.

4. Suppose another catalog has your first item listed for $5.00 less than the price you have listed. A third catalog has your item marked down 20%. If shipping charges and tax are the same, which is the better deal for you, and why?

Catalog Project

1. Find three different items you would like to order from a catalog. Each item must cost at least $10.00. On the back of your paper, tape or glue the picture of the item and its description, or draw a picture of the item and write out its description. Include the price.

2. Complete the attached order form as if you were ordering your three items from the C.M. Project catalog. On the back of the order form, show all the work you did to calculate the amounts for shipping and tax.

Credit: From *Connected Mathematics Series: Connect Math Project Grade 6 Bits & Pieces Part 2* by Lappan. Copyright 1998 by Dale Seymour. Used by permission of Pearson Education.

solver into an interior shortcoming of the student—a failure of character or brain power—rooted in the weaknesses of a student's community, family, or genetic inheritance.

Models of style, intelligence, interest, and cultural difference, on the other hand, take none of this for granted. They view students as having multiple capacities, varied and different resources, and they seek ways to identify and use these resources to increase not ability but performance.

Still, there *are* differences in performance, and the range of these differences present real problems for teachers. How to address them?

By paying more attention to the principle of focused and supported choice.

Graduated Difficulty

In 1972, Muska Mosston, in a book we return to for inspiration and practical suggestions (*Teaching: From Command to Discovery*), made a radical suggestion about student assessment. We can best understand Mosston's vision by imagining a game of high jump on a playground. We play this game by stretching a rope at a certain height and asking players to leap over it. When some can't make it, they drop out, and we raise the rope. The game continues in this way—leaping, failing, and bar raising—until only one player, the winner, is left in the game. Everyone else is sidelined.

In Mosston's vision, this game could be improved by putting the rope at a slant. Graduating the difficulty levels by slanting the rope would allow all players to assess where they could make their best jump and keep on playing, increasing their performance level as they play.

Graduated Difficulty in the Classroom

In Geneva, Barb Heinzman's 5th grade students have been learning how to simplify fractions. One day she gives them the worksheet with fraction problems at four levels shown in Figure 9.3.

Barb tells her students about the worksheet.

All of the problems on this worksheet deal with fractional equivalents but some are easy, some are average, some are hard, and some are very hard. If you had to pick the level you're most comfortable with, the level at which you could show me your best work, which level would you pick? Take out your math logs and write about which level would work best for you.

After the students have thought and written about their choices, they discuss their thoughts, and after the discussion, the students work on the level they selected and use answer sheets to evaluate their performances. Barb then leads a discussion of what they learned from their choices.

She closes the lesson by telling her students: "Now, on the test next Thursday, a quarter of the items will be from each level. What do you think we need to study and practice to make sure we all do well on the test?" The students then slide into heterogeneous teams to discuss Barb's question and make suggestions for the next few days' worth of work.

By incorporating Muska Mosston's idea of graduated difficulty into assessment, Barb has not only learned more about her students' skills in this area, she has also enhanced their self-assessment skills and their initiative and planning skills. They then make suggestions for the next several days of assessment. This Graduated Difficulty Strategy moves through four phases:

1. *Selecting the difficulty level:* Students examine the levels of performance, assess their own abilities, and choose a level accordingly.

2. *Completing the task:.* Students work on their problems, while the teacher observes them, offering assistance as necessary.

3. *Evaluating the performance:* Once they've completed their work, students reflect on their choices and discuss what they learned from the process.

4. *Goal setting:* Students and teacher plan how to move to the next level.

When Does a Ladder Become a Window?

Throughout this book we have emphasized two views of assessment:

FIGURE 9.3
FRACTIONS WORKSHEET

Level I

1. $\dfrac{2}{4}$ =   3. $\dfrac{4}{12}$ =   5. $\dfrac{12}{18}$ =   7. $\dfrac{9}{4}$ =

2. $\dfrac{6}{12}$ =   4. $\dfrac{12}{24}$ =   6. $\dfrac{18}{12}$ =   8. $\dfrac{21}{28}$ =

Level II

1. $\dfrac{14}{21}$ =   3. $\dfrac{9}{15}$ =   5. $\dfrac{35}{10}$ =   7. $\dfrac{33}{6}$ =

2. $\dfrac{25}{2}$ =   4. $\dfrac{23}{4}$ =   6. $\dfrac{33}{44}$ =   8. $\dfrac{6}{72}$ =

Level III

1. $\dfrac{108}{7}$ =   3. $\dfrac{28}{140}$ =   5. $\dfrac{77}{84}$ =   7. $\dfrac{34}{51}$ =

2. $\dfrac{39}{65}$ =   4. $\dfrac{28}{8}$ =   6. $\dfrac{37}{.2}$ =   8. $\dfrac{1002}{2001}$ =

Level IV

1. $\dfrac{606}{1616}$ =   2. $\dfrac{246}{2/3}$ =   3. $\dfrac{153}{187}$ =   4. $\dfrac{784}{896}$ =

• *Assessment as a ladder* (using assessment to determine how close to or how far from a given standard our students' performances are, and what gaps in content, weaknesses, and skills need to be addressed to improve performance); and

• *Assessment as a window* (using assessment to understand how our students think, what interests and learning styles provoke and deepen their thoughts, and what intelligences attract their attention and enhance their understanding).

By combining ladder-type performance assessment models like graduated difficulty with style-based or intelligence-based models that are more window-like, we can create assessments that achieve both aims.

It's easy to see at a glance how the assessment menu in Figure 9.4 functions as both a ladder and a window.

Work is offered at three different levels of difficulty in four different learning styles. Students are asked to complete four tasks, one in each style, but they choose the styles in which they will perform the hardest tasks and the easiest. For example, if a student is most comfortable working in the Mastery style, he will likely be up to the challenge of the level 3 task. Similarly, the student will choose a level 1 task if he is

FIGURE 9.4
ASSESSMENT MENU ON MYTHOLOGY

Level	Mastery	Understanding	Self-Expressive	Interpersonal
1	Retell, in one or two paragraphs, each myth or fairy tale.	Explain what you learned from each myth and why you think people told this myth.	Draw an illustration from each of the myths that tells the important lesson to learn from the myth.	Tell how you felt about each myth and put them in order from the one you liked most to least. Explain your ranking.
2	Use a Venn diagram to compare two of the myths you have read. Describe how they are similar to and different from each other according to the criteria of time, setting, theme, and characters.	Write an essay explaining why people write or tell myths. What purpose do they serve? What are the advantages and disadvantages a myth might have? Why do different cultures have similar myths?	Write a poem of any kind that develops the theme of each of the four myths.	Interview someone the age of your parents or grandparents who is from another country and record a myth this person heard when he was young. Transcribe the myth.
3	Based on your reading, decide what the basic characteristics of a myth are. Prepare a matrix and an organizer to describe the four myths you read and their basic characteristics.	Select a myth that explains a natural phenomenon. In an essay or graphic organizer, use current scientific theory to prove or disprove aspects of the explanations given in the myth.	Write an original myth. It could be a myth from an ancient culture, one from our modern world, one from a future culture or even one from another planet. Give the real or imaginary time in which the myth is being told, a brief description of the culture, and what the myth would help the people of the culture understand.	Choose one of the four myths you read or the "oral history" myth you were told and present it to the class or a small group. Be sure to explain how each character or object interacted in the story to help get the point of the myth across.

least comfortable in the Self-Expressive Style. With student choice focused on both difficulty of performance and models of human difference, the Graduated Difficulty strategy helps both teacher and students understand not only how well the students can perform, but also how their minds work when they are working at their best.

Diversity and Curriculum

Typical high school course description

Traditional Advanced French. This course will complete the foundation built during French I–III. Students will develop their usage, vocabulary, and grammar skills in reading, writing, and speaking, with an emphasis on conversation and reading French literature.

Course description from Phillips Academy, Andover, Mass.

Contemporary French Civilization. Four class periods. This course deals with aspects of contemporary French civilization, such as the family, the school system, politics, gender roles, art, and popular culture. The emphasis is on learning about culture comparatively through the discussion of articles, films, and comic strips. The course includes research on the Web and e-mail with French students. (From Phillips Academy, *Andover Course of Study 2000–2001*. Copyright 2000 by Phillips Academy, Andover, MA. Reprinted with permission.)

U.S. history, English, foreign language, and biology are studied at both of the high schools whose course offerings are quoted. Which one would you rather attend? The difference can be stated in one word: interest. Many schools boil away the flavors and scents that give content meaning into a bland and tasteless stew. Alternative schools—and quite a few good public elementary, middle, and high schools—deliberately seek the spice most likely to give content a flavor that might attract an appetite for learning.

What's more, in these schools students are offered courses that compete with one another by deliberately enticing different kinds of students with different interests and learning styles. Consider these competing English offerings at Phillips Academy:

Writing Through the Universe of Discourse. A course for students interested in experimenting with many different genres of writing. Students are invited to experiment with essays, poetry, literary criticism, letters, autobiography, and other forms of written discourse. Once a week they are invited (but not required) to join a writing workshop with Lawrence elementary school students. This course is designed to serve all kinds of students, but particularly those who would like to gain confidence in their writing skills. Readings for the course include texts from a variety of cultures, including *The Autobiography of Malcolm X*, Haley and Malcolm; *Down These Mean Streets*, Thomas; *Their Eyes Were Watching God*, Hurston; *Cathedral*, Carver; *White Noise*, DeLillo; *The Homecoming*, Alvarez; *I Write What I Like*, Biko; *Sassafrass, Cypress & Indigo*, Shange; *Jacklight*, Erdrich; the poetry of William Blake, Sylvia Plath and William Shakespeare.

Literature of Two Faces. This course studies the relationship between U.S. mainstream and minority cultures, introducing students to the myth, magic, and morality of ethnic identity as it emerges in a dialectic between the community and the individual, as the person struggles to be apart from and a part of larger communities. Authors include Rita Dove, Toni Morrison, Sonia Sanchez, Jimmy Santiago Baca, Amy Tan, Cristina Garcia, Louise Erdrich, Ai, Paul Monette, Leslie Marmon Silko, Isaac Bashevis Singer, Maxine Hong Kingston, Sherman Alexie, Ana Castillo, James Baldwin, Gish Jen, N. Scott Momaday, and August Wilson. (From Phillips Academy, *Andover Course of Study 2000–2001*. Copyright 2000 by Phillips Academy, Andover, MA. Reprinted with permission.)

How different these courses are from traditional high-school fare that offer students little choice and differences only in levels of difficulty, forcing the majority of students into low-level work where neither their interests nor their performance levels will be cultivated.

In the Rush-Henrietta School District in upstate New York, we work with teachers to plan courses and units where attracting student interests is the rule, not the exception. In those planning sessions, groups of teachers work together to design courses like the one outlined in Figure 9.5.

Course developers found that student interest in a course is enhanced if it (1) has a snappy title, (2) the description is enticing and outlines the essential skills that will be promoted, (3) uses a range of texts, fiction as well as nonfiction, and (4) includes tasks that are challenging and designed to pique interest.

A Tale of Two Textbooks

Deliberately designing courses and units to attract student interest easily moves us past the great debate between heterogeneous and homogeneous classrooms. The same principles apply to textbooks. Here's a sample of a typical chapter outline from the Table of Contents of *Functions, Statistics, and Trigonometry* (University of Chicago, 1991):

Chapter 7: Probability and Simulation

7-1: Basic Principles of Probability

7-2: Addition Counting Principles

7-3: Multiplication Counting Principles

7-4: Permutations

7-5: Independent Events

7-6: Probability Distributions

7-7: Designing Simulations

7-8: Simulations with Technology

(From University of Chicago Math Project Functions, Statistics and Trigonometry, by University of Chicago. Copyright 1998 by Addison Wesley. Used by permission of Pearson Education, Inc.)

And here is how the Interactive Mathematics Program (Fendal et. al, 1997) presents one of the five units students engage in during year one of the program:

In Edgar Allan Poe's story, "The Pit and the Pendulum," a prisoner is tied down while a pendulum with a sharp blade slowly descends. If the prisoner does not act, he will be killed by the pendulum. Students read an excerpt from the story and are presented with the problem of whether the prisoner would have enough time to escape. To resolve this question, they construct pendulums and conduct experiments. In the process, they are introduced to the concepts of normal distribution and standard deviation as tools for determining whether a change in one variable really does affect another. They use graphing calculators to learn about quadratic equations and to explore curve fitting. Finally, after deriving a theoretical answer to the pendulum problem, students actually build a 30-foot pendulum to test their theory. (From *The Pit and the Pendulum*, Interactive Mathematics Program, published by Key Curriculum Press, 1150 65th St., Emeryville, CA 94608. 800-995-MATH. Copyright 1997. Reprinted with permission.)

These excerpts are not like the earlier descriptions of the two high school French courses. In our view, both maintain high standards for mathematical achievement *but* each attracts, and is likely to be of interest, to very different kinds of students. The University of Chicago School Mathematics Project emphasizes continual review and strategic instruction mixed with extended applications and long-term projects. The Interactive Mathematics Program puts its money on teams, hands-on labs, and complex problem solving. Why not offer both, rather than no-choice courses that hold some students to high standards and others to low

FIGURE 9.5
THE MIDDLE AGES HERE AND THERE

Course Description The center of our work is a study of three medieval civilizations in Europe, Ghana, and Japan. We will focus on the ways in which three strikingly different cultures developed local variations on a basic medieval design. This investigation into medieval civilizations combines history, literature, and the arts with forays into science and mathematics.

Essential Skills: Reasoning

- Conducting a historical inquiry
- Using literature and the arts to understand the nature of another culture
- Using statistical data to grasp the nature of daily life in other cultures

Essential Skills: Communication

- Learning to read novels and poetry in order to explore the development of themes and the relationship between character, time, and setting
- Developing sophisticated writing within a number of fiction and nonfiction genres: summarizing, character analysis, compare and contrast, scenes and vignettes, poetry and short stories

Fiction

The Door in the Wall (Europe)
Chrysanthemum Rose and the Samurai (Japan)
Tales of Yoruba Gods and Heroes (Africa)
Excerpts from *The Lord of the Rings* (J. R. R. Tolkien)
Excerpts from *Journal of a Plague Year* (DeFoe)

Nonfiction

The Crusades Through Arab Eyes
The Heart of the Warrior
Excerpts from the work of Basil Davidson and Ferdinand Braudel

The Work We Do

- Students keep diaries demonstrating the changes in life across three generations of medieval people in the three civilizations we study.
- Students compare art works from the three cultures.
- Students study maps and diagrams of the evolution of medieval cities and write speculative essays exploring the reasons for changes.
- Students adapt the haiku and tonka forms of Japanese poetry to create journals based on famous travel diaries to illustrate journeys through medieval Europe and medieval Africa.
- Students create time lines to illustrate the relationship between discoveries in culture, mathematics, and science and changes in history and daily life.
- Students adapt medieval ballads and romances to create their own works illustrating the nature of life in medieval Japan and Africa.
- Students adapt the sculptural techniques of Africa to illustrate important ideas in European and Japanese civilizations.
- Students use statistical data to investigate the nature of medieval economies and how changes in the economy affected both daily life and historical events.

Adapted from Strong (1998). Thoughtful Curriculum and Assessment Design (Workshop packet). Trenton, NJ: Silver Strong & Associates, LLC.

standards? Why not offer different courses and different units to different students?

Such an approach is equally feasible in elementary school. When Richard Strong taught at the East Harlem Block School in New York City, groups of grade-level teachers made a habit of designing courses that would attract different students. For instance, four 4th grade teachers would each create and teach two-week units on enhancing research skills. With their parents, students would examine the four courses and decide which course they were most interested in taking. These are typical of their offerings

- *Lions & Tigers & Mosquitoes O My!* Students research animals that annoy, trouble, or frighten us, looking to find their important role in the environment, and then write an argument why we should fight to preserve them.
- *Author! Author!* Students research a favorite children's author—investigating his history and ideas about writing children's books. They then produce an annotated version of one of the writer's books showing the connections between the author's history and theories and the book they've chosen.
- *Civil Rights for Me but Not for You!* After investigating a series of court cases involving the rights of children, students create a Student Guidebook to children's rights.
- *I Couldn't but Now I Can.* Students take a week to work on a new skill: kite-making, omelet frying, fly-tying, bird identification. They keep a journal of their efforts, then transform their entries into an essay on the joys and difficulties of acquiring new skills.

Diversity and School Structure

A final and compelling response to the question of how to meet the challenge of diversity lies in school structure, as demonstrated by the Learning with Style program of Libertyville High School in Libertyville, Illinois.

All Libertyville freshmen take a five-week course called Learning with Style during the second half of their lunch period. Sue Ulrey begins the course by giving students the Learning Preference Inventory (Hanson & Silver, 1991) to help the students and their teachers understand their personal learning styles.

> The initial goal is to make students aware of the diversity of approaches to learning and to give them a powerful model for interpreting their own learning behaviors. Self awareness and awareness of others' preferences, ideas, and styles—these are the foundations the program is built upon. From there, we begin to all work together—students, teachers, guidance counselors, parents—to help each student develop a set of skills and learning strategies that matches his or her interests and that are most likely to lead to a deep sense of personal fulfillment.

Students are taught about the strengths and weaknesses of each style and, using their profile information, begin to design personal growth plans. Along with the guidance counselors, Sue helps students explore career possibilities that fit their learning styles and interests, helping them make course choices that will develop the skills pertaining to their interests and help them meet the goals they have set for themselves. Students map out their high-school careers, meeting regularly with their guidance counselors to discuss and revise their goals in light of new learning and experiences.

To guarantee the program's success, all teachers at Libertyville are trained in learning styles. They work closely with Sue and the guidance counselors to make the best use of the information gathered during the Learning with Style course. Meanwhile, parents are encouraged to attend an adult version of Sue's learning-style course at night so they can help their children and the school make the best choices about what courses and careers their children should pursue. During these workshops, Sue reviews student profiles and explains to parents how their children learn, what they need to be successful, and what areas may need special attention. Sue and the parents discuss what a student's profile means in terms of the next three years, college, choosing a vocation, and becoming a successful lifelong learner who can adapt to new situations.

Libertyville's Learning with Style program is now 10 years old, but, Sue Ulrey says, you'd never know it.

> It seems like yesterday that we started this program. It keeps things new somehow. It keeps the learning environment fresh by helping us to remember that every student has unique interests, talents, and needs and that as an educational institution, we really can treat all our students to the personalized learning program they need and deserve.

Standard 4: Authenticity

WHEN WE FIRST HEARD RUMORS THAT SOME researchers were applying the word authenticity to education, we could barely control our excitement. As students of philosophy, we knew that authenticity grew into our language from the Greek *autarkos*, meaning self-originating, and that it had been transformed first by Rousseau and then by Heidegger and Sartre into an emblem for the fullness of being. Authenticity to them meant a life lived without falsehood, a genuine life built on an ever-expanding knowledge of one's self and the world. By placing a premium on authenticity in education, someone was obviously attempting to think differently about education, to consider fully the question of how school and life are interrelated. But what would these new thoughts mean concretely about life in our schools, where standards rule the day?

For many of us, standards seem to drain the colors out of teaching and learning. As we read long lists of standards developed by experts, the words blur before our eyes. Recent research by Kendall, Marzano, and Gaddy (1999) tells us that if we attempted to teach to all the standards now in place, the average student would need to add five more years to his school career. Think of a newspaper cartoon where the valedictorian addresses the class by saying, "Con-gratulations, fellow high school graduates. We are now in full possession of a standards-based education. Unfortunately, we're 24."

However, in many schools a new and exciting kind of standard has emerged. Here are three examples of this authentic learning:

- In a Manhattan classroom, students are preparing to read Harper Lee's *To Kill A Mockingbird*, but this time with a difference. The question they confront is: How have social attitudes changed since Harper Lee first published her novel? To answer the question, they interview members of their families and other students in the school. They read a 12-part series in *The New York Times* on race relations at the end of the 20th century. When they return to the novel, they chart the attitudes of the characters as well as those of the author. Their work culminates in a series of lessons they design for improved relations among ethnic groups today.
- In Carl Carrozza's 7th grade science classroom, students are studying garbage. They read articles related to a local debate about solid waste, identify the strengths and weaknesses of three alternatives being weighed by the City Council, and write a "white paper," laying out their own recommendations.

• Challenged to identify an aspect of their community they wanted to change as part of the New Standards (Performance Standards, 1997) concern with applied learning, a group of elementary students chose their school's bathrooms. They began by asking key questions about the goals they wished to accomplish. The answers gave them an organized structure for their work, leading to interviews with key personnel and to the distribution of surveys to gather ideas. The students drafted a model showing how all people in the school are involved in bathroom maintenance and discovered problems with bathroom supplies. They used this information to draft, implement, and monitor a schoolwide plan to improve the quality of school life—starting with the bathrooms.

What Is Authenticity?

When we show these examples to teachers in our workshops and ask them what they have in common, one answer comes screaming back: "Reality." "They're all about what's outside of school—or outside of classrooms, anyway." "They're concerned with the skills and knowledge students will need to operate in their adult roles as citizens, workers, family members; as makers, appreciators and critics of art, culture, and ideas— working citizens in touch with the world."

A closer look suggests something not quite so simple, and a good deal more powerful. Notice that in Carl Carrozza's class, learning takes place mostly within the classroom. Little from the outside intrudes; and yet most teachers we interview declare, correctly, that this work is authentic, genuine, real. So a new question emerges: Where is the reality in these cases of authentic teaching and learning? What makes them real? When we look over these examples, we can identify four dimensions of reality, of authenticity:

• *Kinds of work.* In authentic learning situations, the work students do is based on the roles adults play as workers and citizens; the products they create can be used in the real world. Whether these roles and products are simulations, as in the Manhattan classroom where students design lessons for improving race relations, or actually emerge through direct interaction with the real world, as in the bathroom project, the emphasis is clearly on making sure students learn how to produce beyond school.

• *Sources.* Interviews, online correspondence with experts, surveys, City Council proposals, databases, field studies—none of these sources of information correspond with traditional notions of textbook-based and lecture-based learning. They are the kinds of information sources that people use in their careers and lives.

• *Communication.* Authentic learning situations extend reading, writing, and speaking skills in those genres most likely to be useful to students in the real world (e.g., letters, presentations, recommendations, interviews). Authentic communication implies an audience: In most school situations, the primary audience for student work is the teacher and the relationship between student and teacher is private; however, authentic learning asks the learner to consider the ultimate audience and how work produced needs to account for the audience's needs and demands. The audience may be other students; it may be the school or school community; it may be actual customers or clients—people who can profit from or use the work and provide feedback on how well it suits their needs.

• *Problem-based learning.* Problems in the real world tend to be "messy" or ill-defined; authentic learning, whether simulated or real, therefore, uses complex, nonroutine problems to help students acquire skills as investigators, researchers, and problem solvers. Students do apply the concepts and knowledge they gain in school-based settings, but their interactions with reality lead them to adjust and deepen their understanding so that it responds to the real world.

Not every educational activity that appears to take place in the "real world" is necessarily authentic, though. To see why, look at these examples:

• John's cosmetology program has placed him as an intern in a local beauty shop. In this role, he washes customers' hair and keeps the shop clean.
• The Fairwood Middle School has organized a schoolwide career day. Practitioners from a variety of careers make presentations and answer questions. Students write a report.
• Pru and her classmates work together one day each month, cleaning the litter off a local beach.

We can see that this work, though based in reality, is not up to a standard of authenticity. This becomes clear if, acting as parents, and ask ourselves: How much school time would we allow our children to spend on tasks like these? (Students like John may well spend 100 hours at tasks exactly like these.) Yet these examples could be structured for greater authenticity:

• John's student team becomes interested in inventory control for personal products in beauty shops. Working together with owners and suppliers, they study actual inventory schemes and those suggested in the professional literature and design an alternate proposal for handling inventory.
• At Fairwood Middle School, students organize career day. They interview experts beforehand and create a syllabus and a schedule for the day. Using computers, students use word

processing and scheduling programs and create an assessment form and follow-up activities.
• Pru and her classmates have been studying erosion in their earth science class. To apply and deepen their learning, they study erosion at a local beach, interview experts on how it might be controlled, and submit a plan to the City Council for reducing beach erosion.

So What *Is* Authentic Learning?

We want students to understand what it takes to succeed in the worlds of work, family, citizenship, and leisure. We want them to find good jobs. Yet, our curricula and our schools often undermine these desires, sealing the school off from the world beyond its doors. During presidential election years, for example, the average social studies teacher will spend three to four periods on presidential elections but no time on local elections or pressing local issues that offer clear opportunities for student involvement. This isolation of schools from real-world applications also pertains to careers, especially when we compare U.S. high schools to Japanese vocational schools. Outside these Japanese schools it is common to see signs that say, "Thank you, employers, for your interest in our students, but all our students already have jobs." The point is not that Japanese schools are better than U.S. schools, but that they place greater emphasis on the connection between school and career—an emphasis they show by regularly inviting employers to come to school to hire workers. Does the U.S. school system show anywhere near this level of authenticity when it comes to student careers?

From this review we can formulate a definition of authenticity:

> Authenticity is the curriculum goal in which we help students acquire real-world skills and

knowledge by developing their abilities to read, write, solve problems, and apply concepts in a manner that prepares them for their lives beyond school.

Figure 10.1 shows how we can determine if our students' work is authentic.

Why Authenticity Matters

Authenticity and Motivation. Do you remember kindergarten? Do you remember the book corner where you could compose and stitch together your own books, the play money you counted, the large colored blocks you used to build cities, the potholders you made and gave to your mother? Do you recall studying the migration of birds outside of your window, the sand and water tables, the garden you planted that actually grew, the food you cooked with what grew there?

Where did all that richness go? By 2nd or 3rd grade, most students in the United States sit in rows, slogging their way through a world of texts, while the text of the world calls to them

FIGURE 10.1
THE AUTHENTICITY RUBRIC

	1	2	3
Kinds of Work	The roles students play and the products they create have little applicability beyond the classroom and cannot be used in the real world.	Student products and performances resemble the work of adults in the real world and build students' capacities to play real-world roles as problem-solvers, mentors, and collaborators.	Student products and performances are designed to be applied in the real world, and are created in collaboration with real-world mentors, experts, or "clients."
Sources	Students use academic and classroom sources of information only.	Students use sources that are similar to or based on real-world sources (e.g., teacher-designed instead of actual databases) that have been adapted to their abilities.	Students use current real-world sources of information (e.g., interviews, correspondence, actual databases, spreadsheets, and field trips).
Communication	Students' speaking, reading, and writing are strictly academic; the primary audience is the teacher who provides feedback after completion.	Students communicate in real-world genres (e.g., reports, interviews, letters, recommendations, databases, and spreadsheets); the audience is primarily other students but is interactive throughout the production process.	Students use real-world genres to communicate with and receive feedback from real-world stakeholders.
Problem-Based Learning	Student work involves well-defined and predictable problems.	Students work on messy or complex problems that are based on real-world problems.	Students work to create and implement solutions to problems in the world around them.

through the cracks in the window. William Wordsworth, though he dedicated himself to a life of reading, writing, and scholarship, often felt the irrepressible stirrings of the nonacademic world; we can hear his fascination with real-world learning in lines like these:

> Enough of science and of art;
>
> Close up these barren leaves;
>
> Come forth, and bring with you a heart
>
> That watches and receives. ("The Tables Turned,"11.29-32)

Evolution made it possible for us to read, write, and count, but it did not eliminate our longing, like Wordsworth's, to be out learning from the world. By isolating itself, a school eliminates one of the strongest drives to hard work: The human longing to understand, interact with, and even change the world around us. Nothing demonstrates this better than the well-known phenomenon of "senioritis," when students are so busy looking beyond school to the futures they envision that they pay little attention to their current studies.

Authenticity and Learning Style. There are villages in rural Mexico where people make their living writing letters for people from other villages (Estes, 1999). Young children apprentice to letter writers and begin their work addressing and decorating envelopes. Tribal peoples in West Africa, where tailoring is an important craft, initiate apprentices by asking them to iron and sew the buttons on new coats. In both these situations, students learn by doing and observing master craftsmen—not by listening to lectures or filling out worksheets.

Many of our own students learn best through environmental approaches where real tools, real products, and real purposes drive learning, and where adults, proficient in a craft, model the work they do (Lave & Wenger, 1991). In a study of 2,000 students from rural, suburban, and urban areas, Hanson and his colleagues (1991) found that students whose learning styles were best addressed through authentic learning were the same students most likely to be considered at risk.

The reason? As the curriculum progresses toward abstract and academic thinking, students who learn best by working with others to solve the kinds of problems found in the immediate community find school less relevant; they lose their motivation to succeed. The research suggests that many students' cognitive achievements can be improved by including real-life contexts in the curriculum.

Authenticity and the Ends of School. The three million teachers working in U.S. schools represent about 2 percent of the U.S. workforce. The other 98 percent work in other environments. How well are we preparing our students for those environments?

Richard Strong (coauthor of this book) reports that his great-grandfather worked as a clerk in a Brooklyn flannel factory. He spent his days sitting on a stool copying letters and accounts into a leather-bound log. School had prepared him well for this job and with it he provided a better living for his family than his father had been able to. But today's children most likely will not be the clerks, or farmers, or workers on an assembly line that their parents and grandparents were. Successful workers today understand that the global economy creates a world of work and citizenship that is constantly changing, where multiple sources of information need to be converted into solutions for new and unpredictable problems, no matter what jobs they have (Reich, 1992). If the school fails to mirror the world, our children will be unprepared for their post-school lives.

Quick Tips for Increasing the Role of Authenticity in Your School's Curriculum

Making teaching more authentic need not require a huge expenditure of time and effort. It does require an open mind and a spirit of cooperation. Here you'll find 12 manageable ways to increase authenticity broken into three useful categories (gathering ideas, keeping current, ensuring quality).

How to Gather Ideas

Take a Tour. Devote a faculty meeting to a tour of your school's buildings and grounds. Look for the kinds of machines, the kinds of jobs people do, the natural setting, the connections between your school and the outer world. Which of these can be a source of inquiry for your students?

Make a Map. Together with a group of colleagues, map your town or neighborhood. Include businesses, services, geographical or natural features, recreational facilities. Then list skills and concepts from a unit you intend to teach. Where are the connections?

Take a Field Trip to Collect Problems. Select an institution in your town (hospital, historical society, mall) and take your students there on a field trip. Interview adults at the site (consumers, shop owners, professionals) about the institution, their reasons for coming there (including jobs), problems they confront, and how they would like to see the institution improved. Back in the classroom, have students report their findings and look for a service they could perform that is related to your curriculum.

Interview. Build a unit around interviews. Teach your students how to begin an interview, how to follow up on leads, how to probe, how to take notes, and how to collect records. Use the students' interview reports as a foundation for defining community study and service projects.

Exercise the Mind. Barbara Sher's marvelous book *Wishcraft* (1986) is a wonderful starting point for getting your students to think in new ways about their present and their hopes for the future. Use the exercises in the early chapters to help students to think through the kinds of projects that would really get their engines running.

Start with Yourself. Study your life outside of school—your skills, the questions that nag you, the interests you have. Look for connections to the curriculum.

How to Keep Current

Make Time for Authenticity. Authenticity depends on how up-to-date the content of the curriculum is, and what's happening in the discipline. This strongly suggests that we need to provide more time and resources for teachers to study content areas. Providing an hour or two a month for teachers to read and discuss both popular and academic work in their field can powerfully enhance student learning.

Create a Clipping Service. If students—like their teachers—are to keep current, they need new and more interesting sources of information than their textbooks are likely to provide. Can we use our media centers, and our students, to create clipping services that collect new sources of information—both print and electronic, for both teachers and students?

Anchor in Reality. Commit to reading five books a year about citizenship, career, or economic issues that affect life in the real world.

How to Ensure Quality

Organize Product Portfolios. It's useless to ask students to produce real-world products if they don't have examples to examine. If we ask students to create brochures and give them no actual brochures to study—or only brochures

TEACHING WHAT MATTERS MOST

created by last year's students—their efforts will surely lack authenticity and their imaginations will be confined to what the last student was capable of producing. Challenge your colleagues and yourself to collect examples of professional products that can be used to stimulate students, to help them make their own work more authentic as well as more interesting.

Learn from Experts. Interview experts on the standards they use to judge the quality of their own work and the work of others. Ask them to use specific examples to demonstrate their standards. Better yet, ask the experts to examine and give feedback on your students' work.

Jaime Escalante, the Los Angeles calculus teacher whose success was documented in the inspiring movie *Stand and Deliver*, devoted one full class period a week to reports from experts on how mathematics applies to the real world.

The Audience Is Always Right. In designing authentic projects for your students, ask: Who might be an audience? What might that audience want to see? What might it need? Then, create a project or service specifically for that audience and have the audience interact with your students *while* they are creating their products—not just after the work is completed.

Strategies for Authentic Learning

AT THE AMERICAN MUSEUM OF NATURAL HISTORY, television crews were busy setting up cameras and lighting equipment. The occasion was a question-and-answer session between the public and the docent for the new paleontology exhibit. The docent was linked via computer with a fellow researcher who was doing field work in the Gobi Desert. Answering the question, "Why do scientists believe that dinosaurs are related to birds?" the docent explained how both birds and dinosaurs have holes in their hip sockets, how therapods and birds have the same toe configuration, and how similarities in skeletal structure reveal biological connections between birds and dinosaurs. At the end of the session the hall erupted into applause. The docent was a 2nd grader.

How did this happen? Perhaps we should begin by determining what it takes to be a docent. You'd have to be a good student; you'd have to know how to take notes, how to find sources, how to separate important from unimportant information. You would have to know how to organize information so others could understand it, how to speak and write not only effectively but also interestingly. You would need to know how to use media, how to design exhibits, and how to explain what people saw there. Not a bad curriculum for 2nd grade.

Creating Young Docents

Pat Lynch, 2nd grade teacher at Shelter Rock School in Manhasset, Long Island, New York, explains how the session at the museum came about.

> We began with the word docent—an unfamiliar word, but I wasn't afraid of it and I didn't think my students would be either. I've always taught rigorously, so docent was a good place to start.

> For three or four days we discussed our essential question: Can you create a museum and not know. . . ? We all discussed key words and concepts, words like expert, research, reptiles, paleontology, classification. The room was filling up with charts but what I was really doing was modeling how to graph and chart and summarize information.

> We spent a lot of time working on notetaking and research skills. Pat, the school librarian, was a central person here. She taught many of the skills and I only had to reinforce them. I spent much of my time modeling nonfiction reading skills and coaching small groups, usually pairs of students. I tried to place students who had different talents, different abilities in pairs, so that one could coach the other. The

students kept research journals, too. [The journals demonstrate how the students perceived what they were learning.]

Today we lerned how that charts can help us. Today we lerend how to skim. We lerend how to avoid irrelevant, and stick with relevant. Irrelevant means off the topic. Relevant means on the topic. The prosess is going good. Skiming is reading qickly through a book to find information. We also lerend how to use maps and captions.

Today we went to the library and did research. We were taking words from the text and made our own notes.

Today we learnd there are five places to do research. Hear they are inciklapetaea, non-fiction books, computer, vertical file and newspaper. We also learnd to tipto threw the pages and follow the guid words.(From *Expertise. Standards-based curriculum and assessment prototypes, Vol. 3* (pp. 18-25), 1997, Sea Cliff, NY: Center for the Study of Expertise in Teaching and Learning (CSETL). Copyright 1997 by CSETL. Reprinted with permission. For information, contact CSETL at 20 Elm Place, Sea Cliff, NY 11579; 516-794-1211; or www.csetl.org.)

Meanwhile, Pat was just getting started.

Next we began work on interviewing. I wanted students to speak with people who had the jobs they were aspiring to. We talked with both an art and a science museum docent, but only after we taught the students the skills of interviewing and being interviewed.

As we worked, we began to show students how to organize their research into structures their readers and listeners could understand.

I got information on Deinonychus. I made two suborders on my museum plan, Therapods and Sauropods. I learned to make two suborders. This process is going well for me.

We rehearsed our oral presentations over and over again, using rubrics we developed together.

I felt good. I felt like my audience was learning. I think I was loose. I think I was kinda fast . . . I think all that practicing and hard work payed off. I was teaching about 10 or 12 people. I think I developed expertees. (From *Expertise. Standards-based curriculum and assessment prototypes, Vol. 3* (pp. 18-25), 1997, Sea Cliff, NY: Center for the Study of Expertise in Teaching and Learning (CSETL). Copyright 1997 by CSETL. Reprinted with permission.)

Afterward, we used our rubrics, evaluations, and self assessment to discover what we needed to work on. Pretty soon we were ready and that's how Jamie and the others came to be docents at the Museum of Natural History.

Stepping Back

What might you call the work Pat Lynch and her students performed to reach the Museum of Natural History? On the one hand it bears a strong resemblance to direct instruction, especially when you consider the amount of modeling and demonstrations, the sheer number and variety of research skills addressed and repeatedly practiced, including minilessons in the following skills:

- Using the card catalog and card catalog computer
- Becoming familiar with the reference section of the library
- Locating information by subject, title, and author
- Learning about the reference section of the library
- Learning about various sets of encyclopedias
- Finding the appropriate volume for a topic

- Using an index
- Using guide words
- Getting information from charts, graphs, maps, and captions
- Stating the topic and main idea

On the other hand, Pat's approach resembles whole language—the authentic projects, the real audiences, the collaborative work, yet with each student working with sources and topics that interests him. Perhaps the dichotomy between direct instruction and whole language is misleading. But if neither whole language nor direct instruction fully describes Pat Lynch's classroom, what's going on?

Learning Apprenticeships

Before there were schools, the primary tool for learning was the apprenticeship. In an apprenticeship system, a student learns by

- Creating useful products. From the first day of a new apprenticeship, the student is creating products others can use. On the first day, an apprentice tailor sews buttons on jackets, later makes simple hats, then shirts, and finally jackets and suits. Every step of the way the apprentice creates something useful; gradually the products become more complex.
- Watching the master craftsworker. From the first day, the master shows the young novice how to sew on the buttons, how to create the hat, how to mend the shirt.
- Observing other members of the craft community. An apprenticeship community is a mix of individuals of different abilities and specialties. Within this community, the apprentice learns by observing others and by receiving guidance from the adults and other children in this community.
- Being in contact with the public. As Lave and Wenger (1991) tell us, from the first day, an apprentice is in touch with the craft's public. Since the apprentice sews on the buttons, irons the suit, and places it carefully within its box, it is often also the apprentice who gives the customer the product. By listening to customers' delights and complaints, the apprentice learns a great deal about the craft's standards and the public's desires.

Apprenticeship—with its emphasis on meaningful contact with the real world, the creation of gradually more complex and meaningful products, constant modeling by a master craftsworker, and observation and instruction by fellow members of a community of learners—seems far removed from the life of the classroom as we know it. Yet all these elements are visible in Pat Lynch's classroom (see Figure 11.1).

By using the apprenticeship model to ensure authenticity, though keeping central the essential academic skills of reading, writing, researching, and problem solving, Pat avoids some of the most common pitfalls of authentic learning. Despite the best intentions of teachers and schools around the country, three problems often plague authentic learning:

- Content disconnect. Too many reality-based classroom projects treat authentic learning as merely "fun." They fail to set clear standards for instruction and student performance in reading, writing, speaking and problem-solving. In addition, many authentic learning projects fail to produce significant results because the content embedded in the project is weak and not clearly organized around the most important concept in the content area. In a word, many of our authentic learning projects fail because they lack rigor.
- Inadequate instruction. Even where the real world is brought into the classroom for discussion, too often there is insufficient modeling

FIGURE 11.1
PAT'S APPRENTICESHIP PROGRAM

Meaningful contact with the world outside the classroom	Pat's students were connected to the world not only as an audience for their final perform-ance, but through interviews and Internet links throughout the research process.
Concentration on useful products and performances	Pat's students created museum exhibits for the classroom and gave presentations to their parents, but also exhibited their learning to a real audience at the museum.
Modeling by master craftsworkers	Look over the long list of skills Pat and her colleague modeled for the students. Their modeling included the skills and the vocabulary of research.
Observation and instruction in a community of learners	Pat's students were consistently linked with students of differing abilities, with adult masters of the craft, and did research through the Internet, interviews, and through conversations with docents at the museum.

and practice of key skills and few examples of high-quality work for students to analyze.

• Isolation. Too often teachers, in a flurry to cover too much content, see service, career, and applied learning projects as additions to the curriuculum. They assign the projects, but the students do most of the work outside school. Deprived of a learning community with whom they can share findings and discuss both problems and solutions, many students lose interest, founder, and produce substandard work.

Apprentice Citizens

In 1997 the National Center on Education and the Economy, in collaboration with the University of Pittsburgh, published an important set of standards for schools in the United States. Unlike most standards, these New Standards apply to only four areas: English and language arts, mathematics, science, and a new area called applied learning. The applied learning standards relate to student abilities to transfer school learning to the real world; from these come wonderful stories about teaching and learning, like this one:

When a student at a nearby middle school suffered serious injuries in a bike accident, the students in a 5th-grade classroom in Texas went to work to make a difference. Since the newspapers had reported that the boy was not wearing a bike helmet, the students decided to try to persuade the City Council to pass a law requiring the use of bike helmets. They were successful. Not only was their cause reported in the local media, but so was their presentation to the City Council and the report of the bill passing.

When teachers read stories like this we often feel a thrill of inspiration, followed by a flush of embarrassment. Why aren't we doing more work like this? Then we remember, "There's too much content to cover. My students' skills are much too weak. The state standards are much too demanding. And how did the teacher accomplish this anyway? I just haven't got the time." Researchers, administrators, and consultants too often brush away these concerns, interpreting them as signs of resistance. But these are real questions that deserve real answers:

- Was content coverage sacrificed?
- What skills did this project develop?
- If the project was successful as more than a media event (if school content and skills really were enhanced), how did teacher and students accomplish this?

In this case, thanks to New Standards, we can find the answers because we have important clues: samples of the students' work. In the three volumes of *Performance Standards* (1997), we can see example after example of elementary, middle, and high school students' work proving that authentic learning and the academic skills of reading, writing, reasoning, and problem solving are intimately connected. For the bike helmet project, for example, we find student work showing

- How the class brainstormed the questions they needed to answer if they were going to pass a bike helmet ordinance
- Students' progress in learning how to interview and how to draft effective questions
- How students thought through the reasons that might convince others to support such an ordinance
- Students' analyses of model ordinances
- The ordinance students drafted and revised, based on their analysis of models (see Figure 11.2)
- How students considered the audience's needs so that the ordinance would have the best chance of being passed
- The criteria students established for successful performance
- The checklists the class developed to practice their presentations

What this work shows is that perhaps the greatest myth in education is the belief that we don't have the time for citizenship because we have too much content to cover. The myth is exploded from three directions:

1. We tell our students that they need school to become effective citizens.

2. Effective citizenship and career success require such new basic skills as those described by Murnane and Levy (1996) in their research into current professions:

- The ability to read nonfiction, technical, and public documents at least at a high-school level
- The ability to do math at least as far as algebra, geometry, statistics, and probability
- The ability to solve loosely-structured problems and to propose improvements
- The ability to work collaboratively
- Oral communication skills
- The ability to detect and correct errors

3. As the docent and bike helmet examples prove, building citizenship skills also builds essential academic skills and gives students the opportunity to work deeply and personally with rigorous content. But—granted, a huge exception—if experts are permitted to multiply content standards beyond a rational level, they will make it unlikely that our best teachers can teach the skills our students need to become the kind of citizens we hope them to be.

Stepping Back

If we compare Pat Lynch's docent project with the bike helmet project in Texas, though there are clear similarities, the differences are revealing. Both projects involved students with real audiences and real products (museum exhibits and presentations to visitors on the one hand; writing a city ordinance proposal and presenting it to city officials on the other). In both cases, students had extensive contact with adults outside the classroom (docents at museums and online research with working paleontologists; correspondence and interviews with city officials). Finally, both classrooms focused on research, writing, and speaking skills

FIGURE 11.2
STUDENTS' ORDINANCES

ORDINANCE NO. _____

AN ORDINANCE ESTABLISHING A HELMET
TO BE WARN WHILE RIDING A BICYCLE FOR
MINORS; SETTING FORTH DEFINITIONS,
CREATING OFFENSES FOR MINORS,
PARENTS AND GUARDIANS

WHEREAS,   People are being ~~injured~~ *injured* or killed on bicycles each year, in the
United States 8,000 children are killed and 50,000 more are
permanently disabled 75% of all bike related injuries include
trauma to the head, ; and

WHEREAS,   our environment is becoming a risk to bicycle riders, streets
are widening which will increase traffic flow, the speed limit
has increased from 55 to 65 south of _____ and 820, most
families in _____ have two or more cars in use, this increase
the risk to children being hit by a car coming in and out of
their driveways and or neighborhoods, ; and

WHEREAS,   a bicycle helmet ordinance would increase the safety of the
minors in _____ which will attract homeowners and
businesses, this means more taxes, there will be less
deaths.

SECTION 1 – DEFINITIONS

1.   *Bicycle* means a two wheeled vehicle powered by its rider

2.   *Helmet* means a thick covering that fits the head, and is strapped under
the head

3.   *Wearing a Helmet* means the person's helmet is strapped tightly under the
chin

4.   *Minor* means anyone ~~under~~ the age of 15 (fifteen) *or under the age of*

5.   *Private Property* means any property that is owned or operated –
residents, apartment buildings, and business

FIGURE 11.3
COMPARING APPRENTICESHIPS

Docent Project (Research Apprenticeship)	Bike Helmet Project (Problem-Based Apprenticeship)
The project began with the teacher's decision to help her students explore the essential question: Can you be an expert and still not know?	The project began as a response to an event in the community (the bike accident).
In its early phases, the project focused on charting students' prior knowledge of certain key concepts.	The teacher began by discussing a problem with students and collecting their ideas about what questions needed answers and what people and resources could be used to collect answers.
The teacher and other adults modeled key research and communication skills.	Students collected samples of adult products (ordinances, speeches, proposals, and correspondence) then used the Extrapolation Strategy (see Chapter 5) to develop similar projects of their own.
The students focused on developing expertise.	The students' work emphasized problem-solving abilities.

through extensive modeling, practice, and rehearsals guided by rubrics and student reflection. The differences are also interesting and instructive, as Figure 11.3 demonstrates.

Our students need to develop both expertise and problem-solving skills. Figure 11.4 offers examples from various disciplines and grade levels of how to promote these skills.

Authentic Learning and Special Needs Students

Students who need authentic education are among those least likely to get it. Special needs students and students with weak academic skills are likely to be siphoned off in elementary and middle school into tracks where basic skills are practiced over and over again, but divorced from real-world contexts that would give them meaning. In high school, either this basic skills track is continued, or the students

are placed in vocational tracks that emphasize real-world settings but deemphasize rigorous academics. Despite a growing body of research that demonstrates their need for and interest in authentic learning (Brown, 1997; Lave and Wenger, 1991; Resnick, 1987), students with special needs are not connected with an authentic, rigorous curriculum. They may get one or the other, but they almost never get both reality-based learning and thoughtful academic instruction.

But before we leap onto our horses of indignation, let's look at two reasons for these misguided policy decisions. First as Murnane and Levy (1996) show us, all students *do* need to develop competencies in research, writing, mathematics, problem solving, teamwork, error-detection, and both speaking and substantive conceptual understandings in science, social studies, and the arts. Second, vocational teachers and high schools are often caught in a bind: Should they emphasize academic basics or job

FIGURE 11.4
APPRENTICESHIP PROJECTS IN ACTION

Research Apprenticeships	Problem-Based Apprenticeships
In a Manhattan English classroom, 100 9th graders in five classes read Harper Lee's *To Kill A Mockingbird*. This happens in thousands of classrooms all across the United States, but in this case the reading is performed in the context of the essential question, "How have relations between the races changed since Harper Lee wrote her great novel?" This question provokes students into setting up a clipping service on race-related stories from current newspapers and magazines; surveying and interviewing students from their own and other communities on their views on African-American, Hispanic, Asian, and European-American relationships; and making a presentation to the student body on their research and the persistent problems they all face.	In a middle school home economics class in Texas, students don't merely study nutrition, they solve nutritional problems. Teams of students identify problems in their own homes and communities: • Undereating • Overeating • Junk food as an addiction • Hunger in their own and nearby communities • Families that never eat together They use observations, interviews, texts, and online resources to collect information about the problem. They develop hypotheses about the causes of the problem, and formulate and implement a solution. Finally, they report the results of their attempts at solution to an audience made up of the people they worked with.
In a 12th grade classroom in western New York, seniors at a vocational high school begin their senior year studying unemployment. They interview unemployed individuals and social workers in their community; read journal articles on economic, social, and psychological causes of unemployment; and use newly acquired technological skills to create a Web site detailing their findings.	In Phyllis and David Whitin's *Inquiry at the Window* (1997), the teachers explain the year they spent with their 4th graders investigating the lives of local birds. One issue that emerged during the year was forest fragmentation. To help students understand the problem, the president of the local Audubon Society explained and modeled how fragmentation makes it easier for cowbirds to take over tanagers' nests. Students then used mathematical models to explore the relationship between fragmentation and the numbers of tanagers and cowbirds. Using "What-If?" scenarios, students developed a set of potential solutions that they communicated to local experts and to the school community.

preparation? Which is in the best interests of the student?

Ideological pronouncements emphasizing one side or the other, or claiming that one choice will naturally or authentically produce the other, do little to guide teachers and administrators in creating the best future for struggling students. But there is a research-based solution to this problem that our most struggling and challenged students face—the F.C.L.

(Fostering Communities of Learners) Classroom (Brown, 1997; Brown et. al., 1993).

Fostering Communities of Learners

Ann Brown—like Ellin Keene, Susan Zimmermann, and Magdalene Lampert—worked as a practical researcher in classrooms in Berkeley,

California, and Cambridge, Massachusetts. She devoted her life to creating environments where working class students could discover just how successful they could be. Like Pat Lynch, Brown was concerned about meaningful contact with the world beyond the classroom and the creation of gradually more complex, meaningful products. Also like Pat, she worked constantly to model the skills and vocabulary of the craft of research. Brown, however, worked with our most at-risk learners, and incorporated several distinct elements into her learning communities.

Reciprocal Teaching. Every student in a Fostering Communities of Learners (F.C.L.) classroom was taught the Reciprocal Teaching Strategy (Palinscar & Brown, 1984) to learn how to comprehend complex and rigorous texts through the modeling of four truly basic skills: summarizing, clarifying, questioning, and predicting. Key to this process was that, as the students acquired these skills, they practiced them by assuming the role of the teacher, directing while participating in conversations with their peers. In F.C.L. classrooms, once students mastered this strategy they were entitled to assemble as reciprocal teaching groups on their own whenever they encountered a text that presented difficulties.

Jigsaw. The Jigsaw Strategy (Aronson, 1978) was the spine of the F.C.L. classroom. Every student was assigned to an expert group that assembled expertise about a subtopic related to a class theme. If endangered species was the theme, small expert groups might study the plight of reptiles or mammals. Each member of the expert group would then have the responsibility of teaching the content the expert team had acquired to a study team that needed this information for an end-of-unit test and to create a meaningful product.

Seeding. Periodically, the teacher in an F.C.L. classroom teaches a small group of students how to use a particular piece of technology, software, or research skill (e.g., split-screen notes). Having mastered the skill, the students are then responsible for teaching it to others.

Research-Based Technology. Computers in F.C.L. classrooms were networked so students could send e-mail messages to each other when they had a question or when they found research someone else might be able to use. The computers were also used to connect students to adult researchers in the field they were studying and for composing their work. In addition, students maintained writing process files on the computers that included prewriting, research notes, outlines, multiple drafts, stories, and reports.

Balanced Assessment. Though assessment included both traditional tests and authentic products, even the traditional tests were unique, because 50 percent of the questions on them were created through discussion within the Jigsaw's expert groups.

Community Structures. At any time, while some of the students might be working in one F.C.L. classroom, others might be composing or conducting research on computers (two to three students on a computer); studying print materials; or meeting with a teacher for Reciprocal Teaching, the modeling of a specific skill, or as part of a group conference on writing or product development. Several times a week the whole class met as a research community to assess progress and make decisions about the direction of the research.

With all these elements combined with the general model of a research apprenticeship, F.C.L. students showed remarkable progress not only in reading, writing, and scientific concepts, but in the use of complex thinking: hypothesis formation, developing explanations, experimentation, and the use of analogies (Brown, 1997).

Assessing Authenticity in Curriculum and Student Work

TWO OF OUR CHILDREN, ELIZABETH SILVER AND Tom Strong, recently graduated from college and attended a career fair during which they interviewed with several companies and service organizations. Here are two of the tasks they were invited to perform.

> Elizabeth was asked: About how many miles of highways are there in the continental United States? When she replied, "I have no idea," her interviewer responded "That's okay, try to think your way to an answer. I just want to learn a little about how you think out loud."

> Tom was given a 20-page policy paper on hunger in the United States. His interviewer asked him to take 45 minutes to review the report, identify flaws in the research and argument, and decide what the steps he would take to correct them.

It could have been worse. Suppose they hadn't been to college and were looking for manufacturing jobs at the Mitsubishi plant in Illinois. According to Murnane and Levy (1996) they would be hired only if they successfully completed two tasks: (1) examine a variety of machines they have never seen before (what Mitsubishi calls "nonsense models") and the

blueprints for those machines, and in less than two minutes identify all the errors in each machine, and (2) construct "circuit boards" with a multiethnic team. Applicants are given instruction in how to construct the boards, but no guidance in how to share the work.

As we look over these preemployment scenes, three thoughts leap to mind:

- These tasks and questions are all part of an assessment process.
- A person's ability to secure employment depends on how well she performs these tasks.
- Does your school's current curriculum prepare students to get a job in any of these three settings?

Scandalous Ideas About Assessment and Curriculum Planning

Carl Carrozza, a middle-school science teacher in Catskill, New York, talks about his own reactions to these kinds of practical job interview:

> We read Murnane & Levy's *Teaching the New Basic Skills* (1996) as part of our study group on authentic learning. When I came to the

section where they described these new job interviews, I was shocked. These certainly weren't my father's sort of job interviews, or mine. But they made sense. Of course employers would want to know if you could read, write, work with others, find errors, and solve problems. It wasn't just the job interviews that had changed, it was the nature of work itself. We all knew that. The question was, what did this have to do with my middle-school science classroom?"

Then it hit me: This was their first day on the job. These companies weren't using the first day to get them to read the company rulebook and fill out insurance forms; they were using the first day for assessment. So I asked myself, what am I assessing on the first day of school?"

Begin Assessing Authentic Learning on the First Day of School

Begin assessing authentic learning on the first day of school. It's the first day of the new year and already Carl Carrozza's 7th graders are on a field trip:

On the first day I take them on a field trip— to the school's lawn—and I give them a math problem: How many grass plants are there on this lawn?" My mind is full of questions as we begin to think our way through this problem: Who will ask questions? What kinds of questions will they ask? Will they attempt to define the problem, or just start counting blades of grass? How long will it take them to notice there is more than one kind of plant on the lawn? When will they ask if a blade is a plant? How long before someone suggests we dig up a plant or two to examine? What Murnane and Levy helped me see is that all these questions are related to my work as a science teacher. I want to know

- How do they define problems?

- How experimental are they?

- How well can they collaborate with each other?

- Are they able to build off each other's ideas in conversation?

- What kind of records will they keep?

This mini-unit goes on for a week, while we explore issues of estimation in math (how many grass plants are there on the lawn?) and definition in science (what counts as a plant?). They keep daily records of their observations and experiments and write journal entries in which they describe their observations, their musings, their successes, and their failures. By the end of the week, I have mounds of data about my students as learners, mathematicians, and scientists. With this in hand, I'm ready to plan my year.

Sherry Gibbon teaches high-school history in Penn Yan, New York. The state requires a two-year course in global history: 40,000 years on five continents. But Sherry begins the first day by asking students not about global history, but about their own and their community's history.

We had a new mall built last year and I decided to begin the year by writing its history—examining how it came to be built and what effects it might have on our community. I was interested in how my students handled point of view and wrote up their findings. So I booked a week of interviews with people who represented a wide band of perspectives on the mall's history and its effects. My students took notes while I conducted the interviews. This was followed by two days in which we planned how to approach the writing and three more days in which we used a writer's workshop approach to actually write up our history—I wanted to see how they handled the drafting and revision parts of the writing process. On the last day, we invited all our interviewees back and presented our findings and let them critique our work. Then, and only then, I asked my students what they thought history was and what made it challenging. They said:

> History is listening to other people's stories and trying to find the true one. This is hard because everybody's story has just a little bit of the truth in it and what makes it hard is finding those bits.

> At first I thought history was boring even during the Mall Project but then as people began to disagree, like the Mayor and the head of the Sierra Club, I got excited. How come their stories were so different? And what was I going to do about it? That's the excitement of history.

Carl and Sherry, in response to the experience of their own students and the reports of Murnane and Levy, have transformed the opening days of school into windows on their students' individual processes of research, problem solving, and reflection.

Use Real-World Jobs as Standards to Guide Student Learning

Use real-world jobs as standards to guide student learning. After teaching high school English for 17 years, Robin Cederblad of Downers Grove, Illinois, says

> It suddenly struck me that all my work with kids on thesis essays and literacy responses could be seen as a kind of career education, and the career I was training them for was called "becoming a critic."

> At first, this made me extremely nervous. All I could think of was the harshness of critics and the glib way they so often trash good work or exalt bad work. But thinking this way turned out to be a good thing because I began to ask myself what it would be like to be a good, fair critic—what would be the conduct, the behavior of the critic who was making a sincere effort to be responsible? That's what led me to create the poster [see Figure 12.1].

> For me, this worked better than a rubric because now we had a standard to work toward—a standard in the old sense of a banner we pursued. We began by collecting movie reviews of films we had seen and books we had read and staged long debates about which critics were fair and which were not. This gave us a set of positive and negative exemplars against which to judge our own work—and slowly my kids were becoming not just good writers, but responsive ones. Now I'm asking myself about other jobs as well. In my English classes we do a lot of research. So I'm asking myself, what is a good researcher? Another poster. Next year.

Make Sure You Remain Open to Possibilities and Opportunities

In what may be the best book ever written on fostering scientific thinking in young children, *Inquiry at the Window* (1997), Phyllis and David Whitin describe a year they and their 4th graders spent investigating the lives of the birds outside their window. Over the course of the year, their students learned sophisticated scientific skills, such as how to observe and organize information visually through drawings and sketches; how to use observation-extension organizers to turn their observations into research questions; how to interpret complex graphs of practicing scientists; and how to create their own graphs (see Figure 12.2) to exemplify and test their own theories. The students also conducted a critical study of fiction

FIGURE 12.1
POSTER FOR THINKING CRITICALLY

You know you are a responsible critic when you

C are enough about a work to try to see it from the author's point of view, not just your own.

R aise questions that probe the ideas that underlie the author's creations.

I dentify both the literary techniques the author uses and the reasons for using them.

T ake time to organize your own writing so that your readers can understand your point of view and see the evidence behind it.

I nvite other points of view into your writing through the use of counterarguments and counterexamples.

C reate interest and engagement for your readers through your own use of vivid language, metaphors, and distinct voice.

FIGURE 12.2
NESTING BEHAVIOR OF THE FEMALE BLUEBIRD

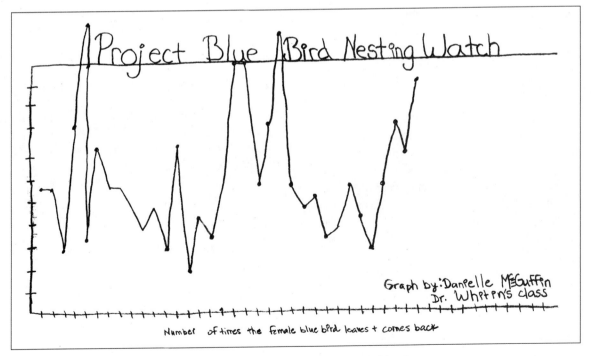

Adapted from Whitin & Whitin (1997). Graph by student Danielle McGuffin. Reprinted by permission of student's parents.

as a source of information and created their own stories and poems about birds.

Much of this student work in science, math, and language arts needs to be seen to be appreciated. The truly remarkable aspect of the Whitins' efforts to strengthen students abilities to produce such high-quality work is revealed in the opening sentence of Chapter 1: "Our year of inquiry began by accident." (p. 1)

The accident was Phyllis's discovery of a discarded bird feeder and her decision to use this bird feeder to teach her students about scientific observation. This openness to the possibilities of learning, and to the connections between learning and life, pervades the Whitins' work. For instance, when one student's writing centered on the word "peck," it led to a search for synonyms and an extended investigation into the use of metaphors in scientific writing. When other students noticed changes in the size of loads birds carried during nest-building and the amount of time they spent in their nests, this led to a "duel of graphs" in which students tested their own theories of the relationship between the two. And when Phyllis's search for relevant materials brought her to an article on how forest fragmentation endangered the lives of tanagers, it led to a visit from the president of the local Audubon Society and a mathematical inquiry into how forest fragmentation creates predator-prey imbalances.

One way to understand this extraordinary work is to say that the students' year of inquiry was nourished by the Whitins' fearlessness. This fearlessness, this openness to the emerging and the possible led to

- Discovery of rich sources of learning (the bird feeder, the Audubon Society)
- Nourishment of student interest (nest-building loads and synonyms for "peck")
- Linking teacher's interest (forest fragmentation) to students' and the teachers' inquiries

The Whitins' work is based on clear standards of successful inquiry, but it is enriched—imbued with the wonder of learning—by their constant search for opportunities to deepen student engagement.

This story raises two compelling questions about curriculum planning and assessment: (1) Do we constrain teaching and limit students' motivation and learning by overemphasizing planning in workshops over the summer? How effective can planning be when we have not yet met our students? (2) How much damage will be done to classrooms like Phyllis's and David's by overly precise content standards in science, social studies, and language arts?

This is not to say that units planned before we met the students are a bad idea. Nor is it to say that clear standards are a bad idea. We are simply calling attention to the way policies and the bureaucratic aspects of schooling can put our best teaching and learning practices at risk. What we need is a new view of the role of planning and standards in instruction.

How to Plan an Authentic Learning Experience

To support teachers like Phyllis and David Whitin, we need a new model for planning—one that is less bureaucratic, less focused on minutely defined goals and objectives and more open to opportunities. To clarify this process, we will intersperse its steps with a narrative by Ann Marie Dillon, who teaches the Introduction to Occupations course for grades 9–12 in the Wayne-Fingerlakes BOCES, New York. Ann explains where to "begin."

B–*Begin by bringing your standards into the open.*

> I began with a simple fact: we've got standards for Career Development and

Occupation Skills (CDOS) in New York State, but most students don't have any clear idea of how these standards apply to them as students, citizens, and future workers. So I really wanted my students to investigate these skills—find out how they're useful and how they're going to have a bearing on their lives and careers. In conducting this inquiry into the CDOS skills, I wanted my students to develop more than awareness; I wanted them to start thinking like people who could succeed in a wide range of careers. And I wanted their reading, writing, and problem-solving skills to improve as well.

E–Establish links to the world outside the school doors.

One of the most important studies ever conducted into the skills students will need to be successful citizens, learners, and workers, is the Secretary's Commission on Achieving Necessary Skills (SCANS) Report. We started out by working in groups to read the SCANS report and extract the skills it outlines. The groups focused on each skill and developed a working explanation describing what each skill would look like in school, in life, and in the world of careers. At this point, students also began keeping reflective journals to record their findings and think through their inquiry.

One of the things we found during our investigation into the SCANS skills is that most students didn't believe that they really needed these skills to be successful. So as a class we decided to put the Secretary's Commission to the test. What we did was develop a survey to administer to local employers, asking them to identify the skills successful applicants would need.

G–Gather resources

As the phone calls and surveys came in from the employers, the students felt they would need a larger pool of data to make an effective comparison between the skills emphasized by local employers and those covered in the SCANS report. This is where the Internet was a godsend for us. Students went online and got other students in various parts of New York State involved in their investigation by having these other New York students administer the survey in their towns and cities. In a few weeks' time, we had lots of data to sort through, organize, and analyze.

What we found after our analysis was that the SCANS skills were right on the money. The question that emerged from this was: OK, now that we know the value of these skills, how do we go about developing them, both in and out of school?

I–Identify skills that need development and assemble experts to help teach them.

Once we had our data sorted, we decided to redesign the course so that students would be able to investigate and develop these skills. Under the heading, *If you want to have a career and not just a job, you need to . . .* we identified some pretty obvious goals, such as

- Become a resource manager.

- Be opportunistic and sell yourself.

- Research job opportunities and skills.

- Work effectively with others.

- Write in an engaging and effective manner.

Students rated themselves a 1 to 4 for each SCAN skill area and worked in teams to brainstorm opportunities for developing skills in each area.

Here's when our contact with experts really became central to what we were doing. We had technology teachers and programmers from local companies working with the students. We had reporters from local papers, civil engineers, small business owners, mechanics, bankers, and police officers come in. Students interviewed these experts on their career history, the skills they used, and how they developed them—but only after we spent two days on interviewing and notetaking.

N–*Never miss an opportunity to analyze adult models and strategies; celebrate completion.*

Based on their assessment of the skills they needed and their experiences with experts, students selected a career they were interested in experiencing firsthand. They set up interviews with members of their selected field and together drafted a list of questions they wanted to answer during their job shadowing. Then, to increase their preparedness, students used the Internet to gather more information about the field.

Once they were ready, students spent time with their chosen employee on the job—taking notes, interviewing other employers, and paying especially close attention to how the SCANS skills were being used on the job. They then evaluated what they needed to do to prepare themselves for a career in their chosen field, and kept in contact with their mentors to help them answer questions, make career-preparation plans, prepare resumes, and develop interview skills.

At the end of the year, we had a business luncheon with career-related, problem-solving activities that asked students to pool their expertise and find collaborative solutions. I can definitely say that these students were prepared for the worlds of work and citizenship that awaited them.

What should be clear from Ann's work is the way this BEGIN process can be applied to a wide variety of disciplines and grade levels. For example,

In U.S. history, a teacher could emphasize

B – Researching and writing like a historian.

E – Forming teams to interview veterans of four different wars (World War II, the Korean War, Vietnam, and the Gulf War).

G – Having each team read one piece of fiction and one piece of nonfiction about the war to better understand the war and the period.

I – Setting up classroom time and field study with local reporters to help students develop interview and notetaking skills.

N – Analyzing biographies and historical nonfiction in class to help students find models and strategies for using evidence, incorporating anecdotes, and keeping the reader's interest.

In elementary-school science, a teacher might focus on

B – Developing research skills; writing scientific explanations.

E – Observing the life cycle of frogs in a local pond.

G – Reading scientific articles to deepen understanding; using student questions and observations to guide further investigations.

I – Inviting local experts (e.g., members of local wildlife societies) to lead discussions and teach skills (e.g., creating observational journals; writing scientifically valid explanations; modeling predator-prey relationships mathematically).

N – Communicating with college and field researchers to help students learn how to use models (e.g., graphs, observation journals, field reports) of practicing scientists.

Becoming Authentic: Howard Gardner's Forgotten Vision

Howard Gardner published a brief essay (Gardner, 1989) that embodied his vision for our schools. Though rarely read or commented on today, we consider it as wonderfully productive as his splendid work on multiple intelligences. The concept is simple: schools are not organized according to the developmental pathways that students and young adults follow, so let's make three adjustments:

1. Since children from 2 years to 7 years work on "first draft mastery" of all essential symbol systems by speaking, counting, drawing, singing, listening, and learning to interpret pictures, body language, movement, and simple arithmetic, *let's create preschool and primary-school environments rich in symbolic media and emphasize exposure to literature, music, math, art, and athletics.*

2. Since children from 7 years to 14 years look less for free exploration and more to selecting their own areas of interest and learning crucial skills and proficiencies, *let's allow upper-elementary and middle-school students and their families to select one academic subject, one art form, and one form of physical training as areas of specialization while they also master a wide range of notational systems and general skills.*

3. Since adolescents from 14 to 21 years direct their attention toward (a) the larger society, (b) abstract and speculative thinking, and (c) examining issues of self, including personal identity, ambition, morality, sexuality, and emotional responses, *let's capitalize on the shift to broader themes by structuring curricula around global, ethical, and social problems and by engaging students in large-scale, interdisciplinary projects that require them to experience and draw from a wide range of knowledge.*

Only in the last years of high school would we make a minor revision to Gardner's recommendations. He suggests a high school curriculum that is broad, interdisciplinary, and designed to maximize open exploration of many topics, questions, issues, and perspectives. We see it a little differently. Our revision springs from a "disease" that is known to every high school teacher. Its symptoms include flagging interest, decreased commitment to high-quality work, and prolonged staring out of windows. Affecting equally the school's highest and lowest performers, it occurs universally between March and June of the senior year. It's called *senioritis*. Traditionally, it's seen as affecting the students. We see it as a disorder in the curriculum.

Starting in 11th grade, students' minds naturally begin to penetrate beyond the school's walls. Ceasing to live only in the moment, they become increasingly preoccupied with their own futures. Yet the school's curriculum plows on—Spanish IV, Calculus, 12th grade English—with little regard for students' concerns for the future. We suggest this elaboration:

3. Since students between 16 years and 18 years have it as their developmental business to begin the demanding work of preparing their own futures, *let's rewrite the last two years of high school. Let's make authentic work the core of what happens in junior and senior years. Let's invite*

employers into the schools to discuss the jobs they have to offer and what is required by those jobs. Better yet, let them interview and recruit our students. Let's do what many private schools do and deliberately create new courses and course descriptions that invite student interest because they resemble college work. Let's invite students out into the world, not in isolated community service assignments, but in whole-class projects where they work together to address the real-life issues facing their own and the global community. Let's have them articulate their political philosophies, exploring party affiliations, from Human Rights Watch to the Young Republicans. Let's have them learn to complete tax forms and to explore the housing challenges that are imminent for them. Authentic learning is the work of the junior and senior years. The future is waiting.

13

A New Deal for Teachers and Students

THIS HAS BEEN A BOOK ABOUT RESPONSIBILITY—our responsibility for the care of students' minds. For this reason, we would like to close with a tale about responsibility and three examples of responsible schooling.

The year is 1957. Richard Goldby is beginning his first year of teaching. It is in fact his first day, and only 15 minutes into that day. At this point, Goldby delivers a brief and most peculiar speech to his 6th grade class. It was called, "You Can Count On Me."

When I was a boy, all the adults around me were constantly speaking to me about my responsibilities. They talked so much about it that I knew this idea of responsibility was important. But one day I noticed something strange. Although these adults regularly reminded me of my responsibilities, they never spoke to me of *their* responsibilities. All the teachers and coaches and my own parents acted responsibly, but they never clearly told me *what* they were responsible for. In time, this began to feel unfair to me. So I promised that when I became a teacher—I always knew I would be a teacher—I would tell my students what I would assume as my responsibilities, so that they knew what they could count on me for. So here they are:

• You can count on me to take your thoughts and questions seriously;

• You can count on me to show you clearly how to do the work I assign;

• You can count on me to help you find out why what we study is important, and how it's connected to your life now and in the future; and,

• You can count on me never to belittle your mistakes and errors, but to show you how to overcome them and learn from them.

Then, only after telling his students—including me, Richard Strong—what they could expect from him, Richard Goldby began to sketch out how he would be counting on them.

There has been great lamenting over the erosion of student responsibility in the last 10 years, and much loose and irritable talk about the refusal of our schools to be accountable for student learning. The talk and the concerns that animate it have led to a new world of standards, supplemented by new state tests and assessments. Both the tests and the standards, written by fallible men and women, have been imposed on schools and their teachers.

Some of these standards and assessments are exciting and invigorating; others are disastrously finicky or vague. Most are bland. But none is written with the ordinary understanding of the meaning of responsibility that Richard Goldby communicated to me and my fellow students that September morning in 1957. Goldby understood that responsibility is meaningless if it is not mutual; he realized that without a clear statement about his own responsibilities, the request for others (a student, a school, a parent) to take up their responsibilities was merely a demand for obedience before authority.

This book is full of stories of responsible teachers. We saw this responsibility when Debbie Shrout committed herself to teaching the same rigorous texts to both her high-achieving and low-achieving students and analyzed her own reading practices to discover what she needed to teach them. We saw responsibility in the math and English classes of Barb Heinzman and Robin Cederblad as, peering over their students' papers, they sought to adjust their teaching to how their students were understanding rates and the concept of evidence. We witnessed responsibility in the work of Ed Wright, who extended the concept of diversity to include teachers' thoughts and their concerns about placing diversity at the center of their work together. And we bore witness to a Texas teacher who, as part of the New Standards Project, sought to help her students find a rational response to a tragedy in their community.

Even if these teachers and administrators did not explicitly describe their responsibilities to their students, their practices serve as models of their commitment to the responsibility of teaching our children. This brings us to a final question and to two stories of teachers and administrators who are attempting to address responsibility.

What Does a Responsible School System Look Like?

Assessment Contracts

In the Cattaraugus-Allegany BOCES, New York, under the leadership of Gail Hirst and Kay Buffamante, and in the Steuben-Allegany BOCES, New York, under the leadership of Judy Ingalls and Jackie Spencer, teachers are attempting to craft shared agreements about what they will be responsible for—what they can be counted on to do and teach—in relation to their goals and their assessment of student learning. Their work is represented by the contracts in Figures 13.1, 13.2, and 13.3.

By negotiating these assessment contracts together, teachers are creating a consensus on what kinds of student work provide key assessment information for the whole group to review. Once agreement has been reached, each teacher selects four case-study students (high, high-average, low-average, struggling) whose work

FIGURE 13.1
HIGH SCHOOL SCIENCE CONTRACT

We agree that all our students will . . .

• Read and interpret articles on science in popular and professional magazines through summaries and presentations four times a year.

• Explore and understand the scientific process by creating their own experimental investigations, and by interpreting and critiquing the experimental designs of others, at least once a month.

• Apply their understanding of scientific concepts by designing investigations and community-service projects at least twice a year.

• Conduct inquiries into ethical issues in the practice of science, and its limitations and powers as a discipline at least twice a year.

FIGURE 13.2
SOCIAL STUDIES CONTRACT

We agree that our students will . . .

- Use notemaking and diagrams to create summaries of important ideas and information they have learned that week.

- Interpret and present their ideas about history based on maps, charts, tables, and primary documents at least once a month.

- Investigate life and learning in their own community, and use these investigations to develop citizenship projects at least twice a year.

- Identify questions and research projects based on U.S. diversity at least four times a year.

will serve as the source of group discussions and planning on how best to help students learn the skills they need. Because all the teachers are working on the same tasks and skills, the conversations and bimonthly planning ses-

FIGURE 13.3
MIDDLE SCHOOL ENGLISH CONTRACT

We agree that all our students will . . .

- Create a summary of a rigorous text through the use of notes, diagrams, or summarizing protocols at least once a week.

- Write an interpretation of literature that includes claims, evidence, and response to counterarguments at least once a month.

- Use research and correspondence to develop and implement plans to provide service to their communities at least twice a year.

- Conduct investigations into the similarities and differences of different cultures' approaches to universal themes at least three times a year.

sions are structured, lead to improved practice, and make instructional responsiveness manageable for all.

A New Kind of Principal

Every month Della Bryant, the principal of School 16, an elementary school in Yonkers, New York, sends the teachers in her school a letter reminding them of the work they agreed to focus on during the month in their assessment contracts. In her letters, she asks the teachers if they need any resources to support their work.

But she doesn't simply send notes. She visits. During that month she meets with every teacher, examining student work, discussing emerging problems, and supplying resources and time to keep the work going.

So many of the teachers whose inspired work appears throughout this book speak movingly of the support they receive from their principals. Simply stated, the principal creates the conditions that motivate teachers and students alike, that allow inspired teaching and learning to flourish or flounder. Della Bryant knows this well, and she relishes the role of helping her teachers help their students.

If you are a principal, we have three questions for you:

- How do you use your time?
- Why do you use it that way?
- In what capacities are you working with teachers to contribute to the success of your students?

In Richard Goldby's declaration of responsibility, the upstate New York assessment contracts, and Della Bryant's regular visits to her teachers' classrooms, we see the beginnings of both a new deal for our students and a new understanding of a standards-based form of responsibility—a shared responsibility that is neither obedience nor a lonely shouldering of burdens. We might indeed call it interresponsi-bility—an acknowledgment that all our respon-sibilities are part of an ongoing, ever-changing covenant we forge with all who share our community.

Teachers often complain that the workshops they attend merely recycle and repackage ideas, with new promotional schemes and new research bases attempting to make the ideas unassailable. We acknowledge the kernel of truth in their perceptions: There is nothing here that cannot be found in John Dewey or Made-line Hunter or Hilda Taba or Jerome Bruner. More important, there is little in this book that could not have been found in the best of the one-room schoolhouses that dotted our prairies 150 years ago or that cannot be found in the best classrooms in the United States today. The point is not that this work is new, but that it keeps being forgotten—not by teachers or stu-dents or parents, but by systems frightened into bureaucracy and longing for the security of established procedure.

The goal of education is not the security of adults and their systems. The goal of education is learning for our children. For that we need to remember the standards that called us together: rigor, thought, diversity, and authenticity. In other times and other places, these standards might have been called a devotion to the clas-sics, a concern for rhetoric and argument, a commitment to cultural studies, and an empha-sis on relevance. The labels don't matter; what matters is that they remind us of our course.

We live and teach in a world of standards, where countless directions can overwhelm us, disorient us, or make us forget our purpose. But the goal of standards is to guarantee that all our students receive a meaningful education—so how do we choose the most important stan-dards to make that goal realistic?

Robert Frost has the answer. He tells us to "take something like a star"—some universal, beautiful, and inspiring *standard*—to give us direction:

> So when at times the mob is swayed
> To carry praise or blame too far,
> We may take something like a star
> To stay our minds on and be staid.

("Take Something Like A Star" ll. 22-25)

Appendix: The Teaching Strategy Index

Introduction

Using instructional strategies to teach content and skills is not some newfangled idea. Socrates, Aristotle, and St. Thomas Aquinas, among others, all understood the need to teach strategically so as to maximize learning among students. A repertoire of effective teaching strategies is one of the teacher's best means of reaching the full range of learners in the classroom and of making learning deep and memorable for students. There are a number of wonderful resources for developing an array of strategies, including Joyce and Weil's *Models of Teaching* (1996); Silver, Hanson, Strong, and Schwartz's *Teaching Styles and Strategies* (1996); and video programs such as Canter & Associates' *Developing Lifelong Learners* (1996), Video Journal's *Instructional Strategies for Greater Student Achievement* (1995), and ASCD's *Teaching Strategies Library* (1987).

This appendix includes some of our favorite teaching strategies organized by instructional purpose. The learning styles and multiple intelligences that each strategy engages are also provided according to the following keys:

Key to Style (matrixes in column 3):

X = emphasized through the strategy; ✔ = expressed through the strategy:

Sensing-Thinking (Mastery)	Sensing-Feeling (Interpersonal)
Intuitive-Thinking (Understanding)	Intuitive-Feeling (Self-Expressive)

Thus: $\dfrac{\text{X} \mid \text{X}}{\text{X} \mid ✔}$ means that the particular strategy emphasizes the Mastery, Interpersonal, and Understanding styles and includes an expression of the Self-Expressive style.

Key to Intelligences:

V = verbal-linguistic
L = logical-mathematical

S = spatial
B = bodily-kinesthetic
M = musical

P = interpersonal
I = intrapersonal
N = naturalist

I. STRATEGIES FOR COLLECTING, ORGANIZING, AND MANAGING INFORMATION

Strategy	Purpose and Description	Style		Multiple Intelligences
New American Lecture	Teacher presents information using a hook, a visual organizer, deep processing, and style questions for processing and maximizing memory.	X	X	V, L, S
		X	X	
COPE	A four-step process for teaching students how to remember information: Collecting, Organizing, Picturing, and Elaborating using memory devices.	X	X	V, L, S, B, M
		X	X	
Main Idea	Students identify keywords used to formulate main ideas and to collect evidence to support them.	X		V, L, S
		X		
Mind's Eye	Students visualize keywords to make predictions, draw pictures, ask questions, or describe feelings before reading a text.		X	V, S, I
			X	
Split-Screen Notes	A note-taking device using symbols and discussion of key ideas and important details.	✔	X	V, S, P, I
			X	
Jigsaw	A cooperative learning strategy. Students work in learning teams made up of experts who are responsible for researching subtopics of a larger topic. Experts from each learning team meet to discuss their findings, then return home to their original team to teach their research findings to the group.		X	V, P
		X		
Four-Way Reporting and Recording	A strategy that uses a jigsaw structure and a variety of note-taking devices for collecting and sharing information.	✔	✔	V, L, S, P
		✔	X	
Power Notes	A note-taking device for organizing information according to the power of the ideas recorded.	X		V, L
		X		
Information Search	A reading strategy that begins with a mind map of what students know, establishes questions related to what they want to know, engages them in reading research, and asks them to visually report the new learning.	X	✔	V, L, S, P
		X	✔	

I. STRATEGIES FOR COLLECTING, ORGANIZING, AND MANAGING INFORMATION—*continued*

Strategy	Purpose and Description	Style	Multiple Intelligences
Command	Students are taught a skill or procedure on command, one step at a time, by the teacher. The teacher then checks and corrects after each step, guaranteeing 100 percent accuracy.	X	V, B
Proceduralizing	A strategy used to teach the steps in a skill by breaking it down into separate actions and then visualizing and practicing the skill until it becomes automatic.	X	V, S, B
Direct Instruction	Teacher models the skill and provides feedback during directed, guided, and independent practice to help students achieve mastery of the skill.	X	V, L, S, B
Graduated Difficulty	Students assess their level of competence by choosing from an array of tasks at different levels of difficulty, then determine the knowledge and skills they need to practice to advance to the next level.	X ✔	V, L, I
Mastery Review	Students assess their knowledge and skills by reviewing important content. The teacher asks a question and allows students time to respond. The teacher then writes the answer on the board. Students can check their answers immediately or look at the teacher's answer for coaching or guidance. The teacher then reviews the question and answers and continues the process.	X	V, L, I

II. STRATEGIES FOR PROMOTING SOCIAL INTERACTIONS AND GROUP LEARNING

Strategy	Purpose and Description	Style	Multiple Intelligences
Reciprocal Learning	Students work together as peer partners on parallel tasks, one functioning as a "doer," the other as a "guide." The guide provides the doer with clues, encouragement, and feedback to ensure a successful outcome.	X (top right)	V, P, I
Team Games Tournament	Heterogenous teams are formed to practice previously learned material. Students then compete in homogeneous (three players) tournaments to earn points for their home team.	✔ (top left), X (top right)	V, P, I
Circle	Students sit in a circle and are invited to share interpersonal information. The leader then asks circle members to review what they heard, to look for similarities and differences, then to draw conclusions about what was shared.	X (top right), ✔ (bottom left)	V, L, P, I
Role Playing	Students assume the identities of others and act out their roles in a scenario. They then reflect on how others think about issues and conflicts, resulting in improved understanding and empathy toward the position of others.	X (top right); ✔ (bottom left), X (bottom right)	V, P, I
I Teach, You Teach	The class is broken up into threes. One person is assigned as "teacher" from each group. The student teachers meet with the lead teacher, who introduces the new learning to the group while the remaining partners practice previously taught material. The student teachers then return to their groups of three and provide input to the other students. The group is then given a task to assess the group's mastery of the subject.	X (top left), X (top right)	V, L, S, I, P

III. Strategies for Reasoning, Analysis, and Problem Solving

Strategy	Purpose and Description	Style	Multiple Intelligences
Circle of Knowledge	A discussion strategy built around a sparking activity and a focus question. Students kindle responses individually and in small groups, then participate in a whole-class discussion. The teacher uses a variety of techniques to orchestrate the discussion, maintain focus, and enhance the quality and depth of thought.	top-right: X; bottom-left: X, bottom-right: ✔	V, L, P, I
Compare and Contrast	This strategy moves through three phases: The first asks students to describe objects or ideas using specific criteria; the second focuses on discrimination, comparing, and contrasting using a visual organizer; and the third is a discussion phase that focuses on communicating conclusions.	top-left: ✔, top-right: ✔; bottom-left: X, bottom-right: ✔	V, L, S
Concept Attainment	Concepts are taught by providing examples and non-examples of concepts. Students use the examples to identify critical attributes. Once students have determined the attributes for concepts, they generate their own examples.	top-left: ✔; bottom-left: X, bottom-right: ✔	V, L
Inductive Learning	Students use the classification process of grouping and labeling data to formulate hypotheses, which they then test by finding evidence to support or refute using texts or experiments.	bottom-left: X, bottom-right: X	V, L
Mystery	Students are introduced to a question that puzzles and teases, along with clues needed to explain the mystery. They then organize and interpret clues to build an explanation.	bottom-left: X	V, L
Inquiry	The strategy begins with a discrepant event. Students collect data using "yes" and "no" questions and generate a hypothesis to explain the discrepant event.	bottom-left: X	V, L
Socratic Seminar	Students are given a series of readings and a set of focus questions. The students then take notes and come together for a focused discussion. The lesson culminates with an essay-writing assessment.	top-left: ✔, top-right: ✔; bottom-left: X	V, L., P, I
Do You Hear What I Hear?	Students listen to a rigorous text twice: The first time to get the gist of the reading; the second time to record notes addressing specific questions. Students then meet in small groups to discuss the text. After the discussion, they prepare a retelling of the text.	top-left: ✔, top-right: ✔; bottom-left: X, bottom-right: ✔	V, S, P, I

IV. STRATEGIES FOR THINKING CREATIVELY AND APPLYING WHAT YOU KNOW AND UNDERSTAND

Strategy	Purpose and Description	Style	Multiple Intelligences
Metaphorical Problem Solving	Students use three types of metaphors—direct analogies, personal analogies, and compressed conflicts—to make the familiar strange or to make the strange familiar.	(bottom-left) X	V, S, P, I
Divergent Thinking	Students generate a variety of responses to an open-ended question or problem. They strive for fluency, creativity, flexibility, and problem solving skills. The goal is to develop an original perspective on the problem.	(bottom-left) X (bottom-right) X	(All intelligences, depending on content)
Extrapolation	Students extract the structure from one content and apply the same structure to another. This strategy helps students to think beyond the classroom and apply what they learn to everyday living.	(bottom-right) X	(All intelligences, depending on content)
Knowledge by Design	All knowledge has a design. It has a structure and a purpose and can be analyzed for its advantages and disadvantages, then modified to improve its use. This strategy asks students to improve an existing design, object, or process.	(bottom-right) X	L, S, I
Task Rotation	Four tasks are centered around a single topic, one in each learning style. Students may choose to complete some tasks or they may be required to complete all four. Tasks may follow an order or may be done at random.	X X / X X (all four quadrants)	(All intelligences, depending on content)
Menus	A combination of Graduated Difficulty and Task Rotation. Students are given an opportunity to choose from a menu of 12 tasks, one in each style and at three levels of difficulty. Students have to choose four tasks, one in each style, and one for each level of difficulty.	X X / X X (all four quadrants)	(All intelligences, depending on content)

References and Resources

Aronson, E. (1978). *The jigsaw classroom*. Beverly Hills, CA: Sage.

Austen, J. (1892/1984). *Emma*. New York: Bantam Classics. (Original work published 1892)

Ball, E. (1998). *Slaves in the family*. New York: Farrar, Straus, & Giroux.

Bank Street College Project in Science and Mathematics. (1985). *The voyage of the Mimi: A teacher's guide*. New York: Holt, Rinehart, & Winston.

Barnett, B. (1995). *Faces of the holocaust: Marcel Jabelot* [Videotape]. Rosemont, PA: Barbara Barnett.

Bloom, B. (Ed.). (1956). *Taxonomy of education objectives, the classification of educational goals: Handbook I: Cognitive domain*. New York: David McKay.

Bloom, H. (1995). *The western canon: The books and school of the ages*. New York: Riverhead Books.

Bransford, J. D., Brown, A. L., & Cocking, R. R. (Eds.). (1999). *How people learn: Brain, mind, experience, and school*. Washington, D.C.: National Academy Press.

Bronte, C. (1887/2000). *Jane Eyre*. New York: Modern Library. (Original work published 1887)

Brown, A. L. (1997, April). Transforming schools into communities of thinking and learning about serious matters. *American Psychologist, 52*(4), 399–413.

Brown, A. L., et al. (1993). Distributed expertise in the classroom. In G. Salomon (Ed.), *Distributed cognitions: Psychological and educational considerations*. Cambridge, UK: Cambridge University Press.

Camus, A. (1991). *The myth of Sisyphus* (Justin O'Brien, Trans.). New York: Vintage International.

Cisneros, S. (1991). *The house on mango street*. New York: Vintage Books.

Collins, J. L. (1997). *Strategies for struggling writers*. New York: Guilford Press.

Collins, K. M., & Collins, J. L. (1996, October). Strategic instruction for struggling writers. *English Journal, 85*(6), 54–61.

Comber, G., Zeiderman, H., & Dungey, K. (1994). *Touchpebbles: Volume A teacher's edition*. Annapolis, MD: CZM Press.

Comber, G., Zeiderman, H., & Dungey, K. (1993). *Touchpebbles: Volume B teacher's edition*. Annapolis, MD: CZM Press.

Comprehensive School Math Program. © Copyright 2000 McREL. For information, call (303) 337-0990 or visit www.mcrel.org/products/

Daniels, H. (1994). *Literature circles: Voice and choice in the student-centered classroom*. Portland, ME: Stenhouse Publishing.

Darwin, C. (1890/1979). The origin of species. In P. Appleman (Ed.), *Darwin: A Norton critical edition*. New York: W. W. Norton & Company, Inc. (Original work published 1890)

Davidson, J. W., & Lytle, M. H. (1992). *After the fact: The art of historical detection* (3rd ed.). New York: McGraw-Hill, Inc.

Dickens, C. (1854/1991). *Hard times*. New York: Bantam Classics and Loveswept. (Original work published 1854)

Dickinson, E. (1961). *Final Harvest: Emily Dickinson's poems*. Boston: Little, Brown and Company.

Du Bois, W. E. B. (1989). *The souls of black folk*. New York: Bantam Classics.

Estes, C. P. (1999). *Clarissa Pinkola Estes live: Theatre of the imagination* [Audio cassette]. Louisville, CO: Sounds True, Inc.

Fendel, D., Resek, D., Alper, L., & Fraser, S. (1997). *The pit and the pendulum: Teacher's guide* (Interactive Mathematics Program). Berkeley, CA: Key Curriculum Press.

From Zero to One and Beyond: Teacher's Guide. (1998). *MathScape: Seeing and thinking mathematically*. Mountain View, CA: Creative Publications.

Frost, R. (1969). *The poetry of Robert Frost: The collected poems, complete and unabridged*. Edward Connery (Ed.). New York: Holt, Rinehart, & Winston.

Gardner, H. (1989). Balancing specialized and comprehensive knowledge: The growing educational challenge. In T. J. Sergiovanni, & J. H. Moore (Eds.), *Schooling for tomorrow: Directing reforms to issues that count*. Boston: Allyn and Bacon.

Gardner, H. (1983). *Frames of mind: The theory of multiple intelligences*. New York: Basic Books.

Gardner, H. (1999). *Intelligence reframed*. New York: Basic Books.

Gilman, C. P. (1998). The yellow wallpaper. In R. Shulman (Ed.), *The yellow wallpaper and other stories*. Oxford, UK: Oxford University Press.

Gilman, C. P. (1994). Why I wrote "the yellow wallpaper". In N. Baym, et. al. (Eds.), *The Norton anthology of American literature* (4th ed., vol. 2). New York: W. W. Norton & Company.

Goldman, S. V., & Greeno, J. G. (1998). Thinking practices: Images of thinking and learning in education. In J. G. Greeno, & S. V. Goldman (Eds.), *Thinking practices in mathematics and science learning*. Mahwah, NJ: Lawrence Erlbaum Associates, Inc.

Hall, R., & Rubin, A. (1998). There's five little notches in here: Dilemmas in teaching and learning the conventional structure of rate. In J. G. Greeno, & S. V. Goldman (Eds.), *Thinking practices in mathematics and science learning*. Mahwah, NJ: Lawrence Erlbaum Associates.

Hanson, J. R., Dewing, T., Silver, H. F., & Strong, R. W. (1991). *Within our reach: Identifying and working more effectively with at-risk learners*. Students At-Risk (Produced for the 1991 ASCD Conference, San Francisco, CA). Alexandria, VA: Association for Supervision and Curriculum Development.

Hanson, J. R., Silver, H. F. (1991). *The Hanson-Silver learning preference inventory*. Trenton, NJ: The Thoughtful Education Press, LLC.

Herber, H. L. (1970). *Teaching reading in content areas*. Englewood Cliffs, NJ: Prentice-Hall, Inc.

Horgan, J. (1997). *The end of science: Facing the limits of knowledge in the twilight of the scientific age*. New York: Broadway Books.

Junior Great Books Series. © Copyright 1995–2000 Great Books Foundation. For information, call (800) 222-5870 or visit www.greatbooks.org/junior/

Keene, E. O., & Zimmermann, S. (1997). *Mosaic of thought: Teaching comprehension in a reader's workshop*. Portsmouth, NH: Heinemann.

Koch, K. (1990). *Rose, where did you get that red?: Teaching great poetry to children*. New York: Vintage Books.

Lampert, M. (1985). *Understanding, doing, and teaching multiplication*. East Lansing, MI: Institute for Research on Teaching, Michigan State University.

Lappan, G., Fey, J. T., Fitzgerald, W. M., Friel, S. N., & Phillips, E. D. (1998). Bits & pieces II: Using rational numbers. In *Connected Math Series*. Menlo Park, CA: Dale Seymour Publications.

Lave, J., & Wenger, E. (1991). *Situated learning: Legitimate peripheral participation*. New York: Cambridge University Press.

Lee, H. (1960/1988). *To kill a mockingbird*. New York: Warner Books. (Original work published 1960)

Lynch, P. (1997). Expertise. *Standards based curriculum and assessment prototypes vol. 3*. Sea Cliff, NY: Center for the Study of Expertise in Teaching and Learning (CSETL).

Marzano, R. J., Kendall, J. S., & Gaddy, B. B. (1999). *Essential knowledge: The debate over what Americans should know*. Aurora, CO: Mid-continent Research for Education and Learning.

Mason, J., Stacey, K., & Burton, L. (1985). *Thinking mathematically*. Reading, MA: Addison-Wesley Publishing Company.

Milne, A. A. (1930/1992). *The house at pooh corner*. E. A. Shepard (Illus.). London: Puffin. (Original work published 1930)

Minarik, E. H. (1957/1992). *Little bear*. M. Sendak (Illus.). New York: Harpercollins Juvenile Books. (Original work published 1957)

Mosston, M. (1972). *Teaching: From command to discovery*. Belmont, CA: Wadsworth Publishing Company, Inc.

Murnane, R. J., & Levy, F. (1996). *Teaching the new basic skills: Principles for educating children to thrive in a changing economy*. New York: The Free Press.

Oakes, J. (1985). *Keeping track: How schools structure inequality*. New Haven, CT: Yale University Press.

Office of the Dean of Studies, & Office of Communications. (2000). *Andover course of study 2000–2001* (Phillips Academy). Andover, MA: Flagship Press, Inc.

Packages and Polygons. (1998). *Britannica mathematics in context: Teacher guide*. Chicago: Encyclopedia Britannica Educational Corporation.

Palincsar, A. S., & Brown, A. L. (1984). Reciprocal teaching of comprehension-fostering and comprehension-monitoring activities. *Cognition and Instruction, 1,* 117–175.

Paterson, K. (1987). *Bridge to Terabithia*. D. Diamond (Illus.). New York: Harper Trophy.

Performance Standards (Vol.1, Elementary School). (1997). *New Standards*. Washington, DC: National Center on Education and the Economy.

Perkins, D. (1992). *Smart schools: Better thinking and learning for every child*. New York: The Free Press.

Piaget, J. (1936, reprinted 1963). *The origins of intelligence in the child*. New York: Norton.

Reich, R. B. (1992). *The work of nations*. New York: Vintage Books.

Resnick, L. B. (1987, December). The 1987 presidential address: Learning in school and out. *Educational Researcher, 16* (9).

Rubenstein, R. (1991). *Functions, statistics, and trigonometry* (The University of Chicago School Mathematics Project). New York: Harpercollins College Division.

Russell, S. J. (1999). Mathematical reasoning in the elementary grades. In L. V. Stiff, & F. R. Cucio (Eds.), *Developing mathematical reasoning in grades k–12: 1999 yearbook*. Reston, VA: National Council of Teachers of Mathematics.

Sartre, J. P. (1989). *No exit*. New York: Vintage International.

Shakespeare, W. (1961). *The sonnets of William Shakespeare*. New York: Avenel Books.

Sher, B. (1986). *Wishcraft: How to get what you really want*. A. Gottlieb (Contr.). New York: Ballantine Books.

Silver, H. F., Hanson, J. R., Strong, R. W., & Schwartz, P. B. (1996). *Teaching styles & strategies* (3rd ed.). Trenton, NJ: The Thoughtful Education Press.

Silver, H. F., & Strong, R. W. (1995). *Reading and learning styles: Building motivation and success* (workshop edition). Woodbridge, NJ: The Thoughtful Education Press.

Silver, H. F., Strong, R. E., & Hanson, J. R. (2000). *Learning Preference Inventory: User's Manual*. Trenton, NJ: Silver Strong & Associates, LLC.

Smullyan, R. (1978). *What is the name of this book: The riddle of dracula and other logical puzzles*. Englewood Cliffs, NJ: Prentice-Hall, Inc.

Stigler, J. W., & Hiebert, J. (1999). *The teaching gap: Best ideas from the world's teachers for improving education in the classroom*. New York: The Free Press.

Strong, R. W. (1998). *Thoughtful curriculum and assessment design* (workshop packet). Trenton, NJ: Silver Strong & Associates, LLC.

Thomas, E. (1999). *Styles and strategies for teaching middle grade mathematics*. Trenton, NJ: The Thoughtful Education Press.

Thoreau, H. D. (1937/1993). Walden and other writings. New York: Barnes and Noble Books. (Original work published 1937)

University of Chicago School Mathematics Project. © Copyright 1983 University of Chicago. For information, visit http://social-sciences.uchicago.edu/ucsmp/

Vygotsky, L. S. (1978). *Mind in society*. Cambridge, MA: Harvard University Press.

Whetzel, D. (1992). *The Secretary of Labor's commission on achieving necessary skills*. Washington, DC: U. S. Department of Education.

Whitin, P., & Whitin, D. (1997). *Inquiry at the window: Pursuing the wonders of learners*. Portsmouth, NH: Hinemann.

Winston, M. E. (Ed.). (1989). *Philosophy of human rights*. Belmont, CA: Wadsworth Publishing Company.

Wordsworth, W. (1883/1984). *William Wordsworth*. New York: Oxford University Press. (Original work published 1883)

Wright, R. A. (1969). *Native son*. New York: Harper & Row.

Index

A page number followed by an *f* indicates reference to a figure.

Related ASCD Resources: Standards

ASCD stock numbers are noted in parentheses.

CD-ROMs
Standards for Excellence in Education (#598337)
Standards Record-Keeping and Reporting (#500347 Windows; 501238 for Mac)
Standards ToolKit, 2nd edition (#599272)
Understanding Teaching: Implementing the NCTM Professional Standards for Teaching Mathematics
    (#597142 Windows; #597143 Mac)

Print Products
ASCD Inquiry Kit *Implementing Standards-Based Education* (#999222)
ASCD Topic Pack *Standards/National Standards* (#197199)
A Comprehensive Guide to Designing Standards-Based Districts, Schools, and Classrooms
    by Robert J. Marzano and John S. Kendall (#196215)
Content Knowledge: A Compendium of Standards and Benchmarks for K–12 Education, 3rd edition,
    by John S. Kendall and Robert J. Marzano (#100291)
How to Use Standards in the Classroom by Douglas E. Harris and Judy F. Carr, with Tim Flynn,
    Marge Petit, and Susan Rigney (#196197)
Standards for Excellence in Education: Guide for Parents, Teachers, and Educators (#198338)
Succeeding with Standards: Linking Curriculum, Assessment, and Action Planning by Judy F. Carr and
    Douglas E. Harris (#101005)

Videotapes
Raising Achievement Through Standards (#498043, 3-tape series)
Science Standards: Making Them Work for You (#495241)
Using Standards to Improve Teaching and Learning (#400262, 3-tape series)

For additional resources, visit us on the World Wide Web (http://www.ascd.org), send an e-mail message to member@ascd.org, call the ASCD Service Center (1-800-933-ASCD or 703-578-9600, then press 2), send a fax to 703-575-5400, or write to Information Services, ASCD, 1703 N. Beauregard St., Alexandria, VA 22311-1714 USA.

About the Authors

Richard W. Strong, Vice President of Silver Strong & Associates, has served as a trainer and consultant to hundreds of school districts around the world. As cofounder of the Institute for Community and Difference, Richard has been studying democratic teaching practices in public and private schools for more than 10 years. He has written and developed several educational books and products, including *Questioning Styles and Strategies* for the Thoughtful Education Press and the Teaching Strategies Video Library for ASCD.

Harvey F. Silver, President of Silver Strong & Associates, was recently named one of the 100 most influential teachers in the United States. He is coauthor of several books for educators, including the best-selling *Teaching Styles and Strategies*, which is used in the Master of Arts in Teaching (MAT) programs at 14 colleges and universities. Harvey is a member of the advisory board of the International Creative and Innovative Thinking Association.

Matthew J. Perini, Director of Publishing at Silver Strong & Associates, has written curriculum guides, articles, and research studies on a wide range of topics, including learning styles, multiple intelligences, and effective teaching practices.

All three authors collaborated on *So Each May Learn: Integrating Learning Styles and Multiple Intelligences,* published by ASCD.

Richard Strong and Harvey Silver
Silver Strong & Associates, Inc.
941 Whitehorse Avenue
Trenton, NJ 08610 USA
Phone: 609-581-1900
Fax: 609-581-5360
e-mail: HYPERLINK mail to questions@ silverstrong.com

Matthew Perini
Silver Strong & Associates, Inc.
334 Kinderkamack Road
Oradell, NJ 07649
Phone: 201-225-9090
Fax: 201-225-9024
e-mail: HYPERLINK mail to mperini@ silverstrong.com